Infallibility

a novel by

Esperanza Zendejas

Ojo por Ojo
Indianapolis

Published by Ojo por Ojo
5326 Whitemarsh Lane
Indianapolis, Indiana 46226

ISBN 0-9670467-1-8

First printing: December 1999
10 9 8 7 6 5 4 3 2 1

Printed in the United States of America.

DEDICACIÓN

To my daughter Baleria and my son Xchel,
my truest love and heartfelt thanks
for your spirited energy and sincere compassion.

This world is a comedy to those that think,
a tragedy to those that feel.

—Horace Walpole

Chapter 1

Agustina sat on a wooden chair at her small kitchen table and watched as the "mad cow disease" court case was analyzed by First Amendment experts. The previous day's announcement of the jury verdict in the Texas cattlemen's lawsuit against Oprah Winfrey was the featured topic on nearly every morning news show. Agustina kept comparing her own personal strife with the battle she had been watching on TV since the beginning of the year. Unlike Oprah's fight, though, Agustina guessed that her own problems would probably never be resolved.

Her eyes were glued on Oprah's jubilant victory smile, played over and over on every channel. It was contagious, and Agustina smiled back at it in spite of herself. Would she ever know the same feelings of relief and certainty? She longed for such an opportunity to tell the world what happened and why, but knew it was too late.

She had meant no harm. She had loved her son with all her heart even though his life seemed cursed from the start. The pregnancy was the dumb mistake of a young woman trying to fit in with her friends, trying to taste a little personal freedom.

Disgusted, her strict and stubborn father, Roberto Dominguez, kicked her out of the house and kept her away from her family and friends. He did what might be expected of any father enraged by his daughter's lapse of judgment, increasing his already tight control of the family. Teachers at Agustina's small high school tried to convince her father of her potential to succeed even with the added responsibility for a child. They knew she was smart and had seen her academic dedication. But Roberto had made up his mind.

It was not until after Agustina's son was born that she began to identify with the tug of pain that only parents know about. She could almost understand her father's grief and the sorrow her mother suffered when they found out she was pregnant.

But now, for the first time in many years, she wondered why she had not stood up for herself and finished high school. Her parents had forced her to drop out right before graduation in 1970, but she thought it was really punishment for being a disappointment to her father. Prior to her pregnancy, her father had always said she was the smartest of his nine children. For years after the family found out about her mistake, he hardly ever mentioned her name.

She thought his embarrassment was at the very core of his anger. Her father screamed in her face several times, reminding her that he had often told other men, "It is not going to happen in this family." Agustina's mother tried to defend her but it made no difference since her father was considered the head of the house. Whatever his will, it was to be followed.

Diego was born at General Hospital in Los Angeles four months after Agustina tearfully but obediently left the family, amazed that her life could take such a horrible turn. Looking back on what had happened, as she often did now, Agustina held herself responsible for her youthful mistake, but regretted even more the harsh punishment she received.

As the television cameras panned away from the plaintiffs' Stetson hats, she wondered how long it had been since she had honestly smiled with the same self-satisfaction that Oprah displayed. *Maybe only death will bring me that peaceful a smile,* she thought. Her attitude was positive, and she always worked with a pleasant disposition, but deep inside her where no one could see, Agustina held a cloud of pain.

Watching the battle for freedom of speech, she identified with the defendant, feeling much like one herself. For so long she had lived like the silenced and indefensible creature her father had rejected. For the second time, she had become a victim of circumstance, this time a hostage in her own home. It was not until just before Diego's twenty-seventh birthday that she began to see a way to heal her family wounds. Because nothing had gone right so far, she decided to forgive herself and see if life would improve.

The cheap kitchen clock on the wall began to play the hourly chimes. Seven bells in the morning signaled the time to leave for work, and although Agustina enjoyed her job, the ringing always reminded her of the realities she dared face. For so many years each new day had brought something different, and most of the time that something was not pleasant.

She rose from the small breakfast table to turn off the television. Luckily, she lived in Dr. Thomas Tonami's guesthouse and her job as his housekeeper was just a few steps away from her front door. Each morning she steamed white rice and boiled hot water to steep the green tea leaves. Dr. Tonami wanted the same traditional breakfast day after day.

Agustina made a habit of taking a long, serious look at her son's photo before she left for work. His handsome young face stared out at her from the frame on top of the table next to the television. She had never asked him for forgiveness. She just gazed at Diego to reassure him that she still cared for him very much. She would not apologize for what happened, because she knew deep down that he would have done the same thing if he had been in her situation.

Next, she stood in front of the Virgin of Guadalupe, as she had done every day of her life after she arrived in this strange environment. The Virgin had been her only guardian and reliable companion for many years. The small figure of a woman dressed in a blue cloak with shiny stars was a source of consolation for Agustina. The olive-skinned patron conveyed such a strong determination for life and love.

Agustina always knelt before her briefly to seek her blessings and encouragement for the day. She knew the Virgin would keep her and grace her with her kindness. The daily ritual of spirituality calmed Agustina's fears through many dark moments. She had never understood why her mother paid so much honor to the saintly figure until she was alone with her herself.

When her father kicked her out of the house, her mother had hidden the small statue in Agustina's cardboard suitcase. She was unaware of it until she unpacked her few belongings. "My Lady," as she called her, had been with Agustina ever since.

The Tonamis had been her only real family since her father dismissed her. Taken in at the tender age of seventeen to care for their household, Agustina had learned how to complete the chores from her mother. She never imagined that she would be like her mother in so many ways. Her mother had been a full-time attendant to her father, catering to his every need, and Agustina was doing the same for the Tonami family. She was there to make their lives easier. Besides, being pregnant, she had no other career choice. In those days, an unwed mother was still an outcast.

At seventeen she could not have guessed that she would

continue to serve a Japanese family as their housekeeper for so many years. She cooked, washed, and cleaned house for them, accepting without question that she was lucky to be there. Staying with the Tonami family provided her with the only comfort and stability she had in her adult life.

Now that the children were grown and gone from home, Agustina had time to think about her life and to focus on the details of her housekeeping chores. Dr. Tonami's home was in the best shape ever under her keen eye. But she could feel the years catching up with her. Her once-perfect bronze skin folded softly at the neck. Small lines winked at the outside corners of her eyes. Her hands were weaker now and when she scrubbed the cooking pots the bones inside her fingers cried for relief from a sharp, annoying pain.

Touching Diego's photo as she turned to leave, Agustina winced at the sight of the deep scar between her index finger and thumb. It always reminded her of the many problems they faced together, and of the real connection to danger she had often felt in his presence.

But it was a bright, sunny Los Angeles day as she passed through the garden and into Dr. Tonami's home. The scent of the main house always made her smile. The cherry wood on the walls exuded a distinct forest-like aroma. The tatami mats on the floor and the numerous pieces of furniture and pottery imported from Japan added to the unique Oriental flavor of the environment. To Agustina, it was a totally different world. Yet she knew the home so well she could close her eyes and walk from room to room without tripping on a mat or bumping into the low tables.

She could hear the shower running upstairs. Dr. Tonami was preparing for work. A wise man in his late fifties, he was Agustina's most trusted friend. He had been there for her when she needed him the most. She missed her son very much, and Dr. Tonami mourned his wife. They balanced each other, connected in their sorrows. Actually, she thought, Dr. Tonami was her only friend. When Diego became hard to manage she had given up on having any social life.

Dr. Tonami was a UCLA-trained pathologist. A well-known and respected doctor, he was often called to testify in court cases about cause of death. After a highly publicized case, TV crews hounded him for interviews, but he rarely spoke about his work — in public or at home. He spent many of his working hours researching information in his private library off the living room. Occasionally

Agustina learned about a case because she peeked at the
evidence exhibits full of gruesome, full-color crime photos.

She sensed that today he was going to be involved in
something very important. Yesterday he had left behind a
handwritten note on his bedroom night stand. Normally,
he brought his notes to the breakfast table in order to let
Agustina know which suit and shirt he needed for the following day. Agustina carefully chose a tie for him each
morning, something his wife had always done until cancer
had kept her bedridden.

When Mrs. Tonami passed away and the responsibility
became Agustina's, she prayed to the Virgin that she
could learn how to match clothes. She had no experience
with shirts and ties and was worried that she might not do
a good job. Dr. Tonami never complained. Agustina wasn't
sure if he was just being polite or if he really couldn't see
the difference, but she always thanked the Virgin Mother
for helping her.

As usual, she turned the radio dial to her favorite Mexican
music program, a daily habit before preparing the morning
meal. She enjoyed listening to the same songs her parents
had always played at five o'clock each morning before her
father went to work at Dr. Tonami's father's farm in the

Imperial Valley. The radio was her only connection to them, as well as her only contact with her native language. English and Japanese were spoken in the Tonami home; conversations in Spanish were rare.

As she washed the rice she looked around the empty kitchen. Not having anyone around the house all day gave her too much time to dwell on her insecurities and worry about her limitations as a human being.

She had never stopped being lonely since that spring day many years ago when she arrived five months' pregnant. The Tonami home was lovely and the surroundings were beautiful but Agustina could feel an emptiness deep inside her. The house was surrounded by trees and lush vegetation that made her feel far away from her real home, and a light but desolate fog often hung over the place.

Dr. Tonami's family had put in many imported tropical plants on all sides of the Japanese-style house. Nearby, a small plot was devoted to the Oriental vegetable garden that grew year-round. On the east side of the yard, a small greenhouse stood about thirty feet from the house. Inside the controlled environment, orchid branches spilled through ornamental trees and native Japanese plants. The bulbs were hidden among large plants resembling banana trees, whose long green fronds drooped down over the smaller plants. A small area had been set aside for a bonsai collection, and nestled in one of the corners was a special plot filled with herbs Agustina used in her folk medicines. She was responsible for the plants inside the house, but once a week a Japanese gardener worked in the greenhouse and tended to the outdoor plants. Agustina thought the fresh vegetables from the Tonami garden were the best she'd ever eaten.

A peaceful pond was the centerpiece in another large garden to the north. It was surrounded by marsh grasses and black, slippery rocks. Goldfish and koi swam gracefully through the cool water, flashing red and gold. Another, smaller pond flowed through a waterfall into the larger pool, where several varieties of pink waterlilies bloomed night and day. Trails made from large flat stones wound from home to pond and from pond to resting benches under the apricot trees.

Agustina spent lots of time outside. Whenever her loneliness overwhelmed her, the fish swimming in the pond and the fragrant green gardens comforted her. She believed that she had developed a personal relationship with the koi, who blew kisses to her with their red-and-black lips when she fed them. Like children, they pushed each other and bickered over the first morsel of food.

Dr. Tonami joined Agustina in the kitchen for breakfast, sitting at a traditional Japanese table whose legs rose just a foot from the floor. He always sat facing the large window that overlooked the water garden. Even at this hour, the sun was already drying the dew on the plants. It seemed to Agustina that the sun visited the Tonami garden early to get its first drink of water on a hot day.

Dr. Tonami enjoyed the morning view immensely. His own grandfather had taken breakfast by a window in the "land of the rising sun," so this morning ritual kept the old ways alive.

When Dr. Tonami said "Good morning," he meant it. He never said that when gray skies greeted him at breakfast. On those days, he asked Agustina if she could help the sun peep through the thickness of the clouds. He often recalled visits to his ancestral home on the southeastern coast of Japan, and reminded Agustina that the sun always visited Japan first. She teased him that even if it appeared first in Japan, it lasted the longest overlooking the Imperial Valley. He laughed, knowing well the heat in the California desert where his father's farm was.

When Agustina first arrived to help the Tonamis, she tried sitting at the Japanese table, but it was too low for her. Besides, her protruding abdomen kept her too far away to eat easily. She never understood why the low table was so comfortable for the family. But she had learned to mind her own business, and chose cozier furnishings for the small guesthouse. It was more important to her that Dr. Tonami trusted and valued her. He was the only man she had ever trusted.

• • •

JAPANESE FAMILIES FIRST IMMIGRATED to southeastern California's Imperial Valley in the late 1800s, when the U.S. government's Chinese Exclusion Act made cheap foreign labor hard to find. Most Issei — first generation Japanese immigrants — worked in the timber and fishing industries or for the railroads, saving their earnings in order to lease unwanted tracts of arid land for growing "truck gardens" — produce to be sold at local markets that wouldn't compete with the row crops grown by Anglos. Japanese families who had worked in the sugar-beet fields and as rail laborers knew that the "winter salad bowl" — the hot desert area bordering Arizona and Mexico — offered rich soil and plenty of water from the Colorado River. Among these immigrants was Dr. Thomas

Tonami's grandfather. Like many others, he had arrived in the Valley from Japan via San Francisco in the 1890s, and labored laying tracks for the railroads. He encouraged his own sons to study agriculture; the eldest, Takuichi, was interested in plants and apprenticed himself to an Anglo farmer in the Imperial Valley.

In 1935 Takuichi married Flora Ikeda, and by 1940 they had two sons, Frank and Thomas. Takuichi worked a few years as a farm hand in the Valley before he leased his own 2,500 acres. The business was profitable enough that they also planted experimental cantaloupe and cotton crops along with vegetables. The family's successful endeavors provided opportunities for other immigrants to follow the Japanese pioneers.

Roberto and Altagracia Dominguez immigrated to the Imperial Valley from central Mexico just east of the Sierra Madre in 1935. The United States was recovering from the Great Depression, and agriculture prices and wages were increasing. The possibility of jobs and security gave the young couple the incentive to move north in search of work. Roberto joined other Mexican men to work on the Tonami farm a month after their arrival in the hot, dry desert. Altagracia gave birth to their first son in the new country.

Tonami monitored his farming business like a hawk flying silently over prey. He noted Dominguez's work ethic and efficiency. It was not difficult to distinguish the strong bodies of Roberto and his friends since most of the Mexicans looked scraggly and hungry. To a man as short as Takuichi Tonami, Roberto Dominguez stood out like a tall Saguaro cactus in the middle of the desert. Tonami saw that this particular worker never slowed down and was a leader among the others.

Not long after, Tonami invited Dominguez to supervise the field workers. Most of the men were Mexican and Filipino immigrants and a few were Japanese. Roberto was very happy with his new employment arrangement as it provided security for his wife and their growing family.

Tonami knew that other farmers would soon offer Roberto better work opportunities. It was common to have his best employees enticed away to other jobs. Tonami wanted to keep his right-hand-man close to the farm, so he built a small house for Roberto next to his own spacious home. He hoped this effort would keep the Dominguez family together and near.

The little house brought the Dominguez family much happiness. They were extremely grateful for the opportunity to have a place of their own with amenities far superior to what they had had before. Because of it they welcomed the arrival of a new baby each year.

The Dominguez and Tonami families depended on each other for support and help. Altagracia Dominguez helped the Tonami family with their housekeeping chores while she maintained her own household, including responsibility for five children and a demanding husband. The Tonami boys and the Dominguez boys played and attended an immigrant school together.

Perhaps the glue that initially bonded the families was the realization that they were all immigrants in a time when new arrivals from non-European countries were unpopular. But the business of agriculture did not give much time for them to analyze the intolerant behaviors of many already living in the melting pot. Their work was constant and did not allow for distractions like politics. The hot sun seemed to dry up worldly issues before they had a chance to reach the Imperial Valley.

Then in 1941 Japan bombed the U.S. military base at Pearl Harbor, and life swiftly took on political meaning for the Tonamis and other individuals of Japanese descent living in the United States.

President Roosevelt declared war on Japan. Threatened by the surprise attack and fearing additional warfare closer to home, the Congress requested and received authorization to evacuate all Japanese from the West Coast states. By February 1942, the Tonami family had no choice but to leave the Imperial Valley or be detained in a camp. They were devastated by the punishment they faced as perceived enemies of their adopted country.

It was at this point that the bond between the Tonami and Dominguez families was permanently fixed, and the Tonamis became indebted to Agustina's father and her family.

Roberto Dominguez could not bear to see Takuichi Tonami desert his home or sell at a loss like many Japanese farmers were doing. He approached his boss with a generous plan.

"Takuichi, why don't you move to Mexico until this whole mess is over?" he suggested after seeing the Japanese family begin to pack their belongings. "I can take care of the farm for a while. You can be over the border in one hour."

Tonami was hesitant but his other choices were more painful. The government's relocation centers were too far away from the Imperial Valley for him to manage his farm from a distance. And he was already hearing of resentment toward Japanese families who had moved to the Midwest.

Quietly, the Japanese family continued packing their reed suitcases in preparation for an unknown destination. The children of both families were confused by the grief they saw. The anxiety formed aging lines on the faces of Takuichi and Flora Tonami almost overnight. The government would soon force their evacuation.

At last Tonami accepted the kind offer from his field supervisor. Within a week, Dominguez helped the Tonamis relocate to his own home village in south-central Mexico, where he knew they would be safe. Tonami was concerned about the move, but his family's unity came first. He had already heard from other Japanese farmers that the American government isolated relatives from each other in distant internment camps, and he could not stand to be separated from his wife and children.

Roberto and his seven-year-old son accompanied the Tonamis on the long train ride to the mountainous village of La Flor. The village was remote and had no modern amenities like the family enjoyed in Imperial Valley. The

green mountains reminded Takuichi of his homeland in
Japan, but differences were noticeable, too. Mexicans in
this part of the country did not grow rice. Instead, corn
was the main staple, along with beans and squash. The
villagers ate with tortillas, using them as their utensils
instead of chopsticks for picking up bites of food. But
these differences were minor and Tonami was sure that he
and his family could adapt just as they had in the United
States.

Dominguez introduced the Tonamis to all his relatives,
assuring the Japanese family that their safety would be
guaranteed. The small village reminded Takuichi and
Flora of life in Japan. The homes were similarly construct-
ed and the people were also small-framed and friendly.

The Tonamis' departure brought major transitions for the
Dominguezes in the following several years. Roberto and
Altagracia took care of the farm and the Tonamis'
Japanese house while their older children took care of the
younger ones. Roberto felt sure that the war would end
and the relocation program would not last.

Meanwhile his responsibilities tripled. His commitment to
Takuichi was solid and he worked extra hours to maintain
the property in good working order. In despair over the

forced evacuation, many Japanese farmers had sold their cars and other valuables for pennies on the dollar. Selfish people cashed in on their misfortune and quickly took over properties as soon as they were vacated. But the Dominguez family refused to participate and instead concentrated on maintaining the Tonami farm in the best possible condition.

Before the family departed for Mexico, Tonami had temporarily transferred all his assets to Dominguez's oldest son, Macario, to make sure that the American government did not take his land for other farmers to use. Though Macario was just a child, as a second-generation Mexican-American immigrant born in the United States, he could legally own land. Tonami also left a financial budget for his farm, hoping to secure the ongoing operations so that Roberto could work without interruption. The Japanese farmer trusted his foreman to handle the business. Dominguez knew every detail of the farm and Tonami had instilled in him an unbreakable confidence in its operation.

When the crisis finally ended in 1945, the Tonamis returned to their farm and the Dominguezes, now with three additional children, were very happy to see them. Each family had suffered from the other's absence.

Tonami carefully inspected all of his farmland and found it better than he had left it. The restitution of his land and belongings was immediate. It had never occurred to Dominguez to ask for any compensation. Tonami had read him well: Roberto was honest and loyal.

Dominguez's limited English made communication somewhat difficult but Takuichi showed great patience as his Mexican friend enthusiastically reported on the growth of the farm. Dominguez knew many words in English but had a difficult time phrasing them in the proper order when he was excited. Altagracia spoke only Spanish, yet the two families seemed to understand each other perfectly well after their long separation.

The Tonamis felt indebted to the Dominguezes in many ways. They gave gifts and provided bonuses to Roberto and his family, and their unspoken appreciation was always apparent. Dominguez was glad to continue as foreman and second in command of the farm. Because the Dominguez family had grown so large during his absence, Tonami added two more rooms to the guesthouse and put the small piece of property in Macario Dominguez's name permanently. Roberto was grateful for the unexpected reward.

2

Chapter 2

As Dr. Tonami drank his tea, his eyes followed Agustina as if he knew her deepest secrets.

"Do you have much work today?" she asked him. It was the same question she had asked every morning since his wife had died.

"I'm going to Ventura County to work on a murder case," he said matter-of-factly. He exercised the chopsticks between his fingers for a few seconds, then lifted the bowl close to his mouth. For a quick moment, his eyes focused on the long grains. Then lightly and skillfully he used the wooden sticks to scoop the steaming rice into his mouth. Agustina had fried some chiles for him, too. As a young boy exiled in Mexico during the war, he had learned to mix bits of hot red peppers with his rice. When he was finished he stacked his dishes carefully and thanked Agustina with a formal bow of his head.

"I'll be staying overnight for this case," Dr. Tonami added as he lifted his light frame from the floor, and then returned to his room to pack. Agustina knew that right before he left he would ask if she needed anything. He always wanted to be sure she had any help she might want. But she never interrupted the flow of his day with talk of household matters. Usually, she tried to fix what she could herself or called Pedro, the handyman, to help her with any major repairs.

Reappearing with his garment bag and briefcase, Dr. Tonami slipped into comfortable driving shoes and left for the two-hour drive to Ventura. Agustina wondered if he had a girlfriend. Lately, he'd been staying overnight some-where several times a week. Her mind danced inquisitive-ly with the possibility. Occasionally, he brought a guest home and Agustina prepared an elaborate meal for din-ner. She wondered if the next guest might be his next wife.

Today, she'd dust the library and the furniture, she thought. This would be a good opportunity since she didn't have to cook dinner. She could move a little slower than usual on such an easy day.

After washing the few dishes and tidying the kitchen, Agustina sat quietly in Dr. Tonami's library. The smell of old leather-covered medical books on teak bookshelves mesmerized her. This room had always been her favorite place in the entire house, because she felt that it somehow supported her once-academically active mind. It was also her favorite because of its small size. Dusting was a simple chore. But most important, she could pull books out and learn things she'd never known before. It always made her wish that she had finished high school.

The humble tatami mats on the floor lightened the weight of a room filled with scientific reference books and journals. A skull sat silently at eye level across from Agustina. Though the vacant piece of medical evidence had unnerved her the first time she saw it, she came to respect it as an example of the human species. On the east side of the library, a large bronze sculpture of Darwin rested on a tall, narrow stand.

Every morning the sun rose over Darwin's head and sent its beams across the matted floor. Tiny dust particles floated in the air around Darwin and settled on his nose and hands. Agustina kept the meditative figure as clean as she could. If she did not, the sun rays would tell on her.

She often wondered if Darwin would be proud of her for taking care of his likeness. She distantly remembered high school classroom discussions on Darwin but realized she had now spent more time dusting him than she ever had learning about his theories.

After preparing and serving dinner, Agustina always went to the library to pick up and shelve any books that had been left out. Dr. Tonami had carefully taught her the system by which he wanted his books filed. At first she had rejected his instructions because she thought they were beyond her abilities, but after a few practice sessions she quickly learned his rules. She realized that shelving books was similar to washing bed sheets, folding and putting them away properly. The kitchenware and the wine glasses also had their own filing systems. Thinking this way had made it easier for her to learn.

The books had intimidated her at first; another opportunity on hold because of her greater priorities. Her pregnancy and her household chores were all she could manage. Later, the books had become her dear companions. Whenever possible, Agustina sat as she was sitting now, reading until her eyes watered with fatigue. The library consoled her.

When she couldn't read another word, she shifted her gaze to the photos on the walls of Dr. Tonami's sons as they were growing up. The family had always invited Diego on their outings, and one of the photos included him. She carefully removed the frame from its hook to hold the picture Dr. Tonami took when they visited the Long Beach boardwalk. The three children loved the amusement park. Diego, Tom Jr., and Bob were all smiles. The Japanese boys were older than Diego but always treated him with dignity and respect.

The memory was bittersweet for Agustina, as the photo had been taken about the same time Diego started hanging around other boys who influenced him in the wrong direction. She still blamed them for the start of Diego's problems. He had been a good son who did well in school until he met up with them.

Because she hadn't known his father well, she attributed Diego's personality traits to the influence of other family members. She thought that he was smart and bullheaded like her own father, his grandfather. She hoped that he would be better educated than her family was, though. The Tonamis had given her many books to study and children's books to read while she was pregnant. Before Diego was born, she had practiced reading the children's books, hoping that her unborn baby was listening.

Diego was named after an Aztec peasant boy who was blessed by the Virgin of Guadalupe in Mexico City. The Patron Saint of Mexicans appeared before Juan Diego in the hills and gave him instructions to find the priest and tell him that a church must be built on the hill. Diego was a good child, and he obeyed the Virgin. But the priest did not believe the Indian boy's apparition story. The Virgin of Guadalupe appeared before Diego again and asked him to pick some wild roses for the priest. Ever obedient, the boy gathered as many of the fragrant flowers as he could, carrying them close to his chest in the hem of his shirt. In the presence of the priest, Diego dropped the roses from his clothing and a perfect picture of the Virgin had been miraculously painted on his shirt. The astonished priest knew then that the boy was truthful.

Agustina was so glad that Pope John Paul had beatified Juan Diego for sainthood. This inspired her faith in "her Lady" more than ever.

She decided to name her baby after the peasant boy who carried flowers to the priest. The Virgin had given her so much strength during her pregnancy that she thought it would be an appropriate way to honor the saint and insure blessings for her new son. But life has a way of twisting things cruelly.

She held the picture of the three boys next to her chest as if she wanted Diego to hear her heartbeat. She closed her eyes and settled back into the soft leather couch, her eyes welling with the painful memories.

• • •

IN 1981, AGUSTINA HAD BEEN TOTALLY SURPRISED by a phone call from the principal at Diego's school. Her son was going to be expelled for doing something so terrible that the principal would not even discuss it on the phone. She was expected to pick up Diego immediately. Mrs. Tonami had overheard the conversation and knew that something was wrong. She insisted on driving Agustina to the school, and they rushed out of the house. Agustina's mind began to race with anxiety. If the principal was so upset, Diego must have done something unbelievably bad. Not until many years later did Agustina realize that she had reacted like her own parents would have. "If you get in trouble at school, you will be in trouble at home," her father often told all of the Dominguez children.

Mrs. Tonami dropped Agustina at the front door of the school. In the principal's office were four boys including Diego, waiting for anxious parents to arrive. The principal informed Agustina that Diego and his three older friends had damaged the boys' restroom. She could not believe that Diego would do such a thing. Her son knew that she worked as a housekeeper and that cleaning was a difficult chore. Why would her son make a mess on purpose? Agustina was embarrassed and puzzled.

The principal took her to the restroom to show her what had happened. There were large, wet paper wads on the ceiling and mirrors, still dripping with water. Toilet paper rolls were scattered as if the culprits had tried to carpet the floor with them. The metal doors had been kicked until they caved in, and a sharp object had been used to scar them beyond repair. Graffiti had been drawn all over the walls with permanent markers.

But the worst part literally took Agustina's breath away. The boys had spread feces on the walls inside one of the stalls. Her son would not do this, she thought. There had been some mistake. Diego would tell her what had happened.

Outside the principal's office, she spent two minutes with her son.

"Diego, did you make that mess in the bathroom?" She looked hard at him, hoping that a negative answer would leave his lips. Diego hung his head. "Look at me!" She grabbed him by his shoulders and forced him to face her. His resentment flowed through her hands and pierced her heart. She had never felt such anger from him, and knew immediately that he would lie to her. Diego pulled away defiantly and turned his head to hide his tears. This was not the son she knew. Something was wrong.

Stepping into the hallway, the principal told Agustina that the older boys were leading Diego. He called it "peer pressure." She had brought Diego up to be confident and self-reliant, so the principal's words were offensive and confusing.

No matter which boy had led the way, it was evident to Agustina that her son was involved in the stupid but very serious game of vandalism. For defacing school property Diego and the other boys were suspended for five days.

Mrs. Tonami drove Agustina and Diego home in silence. Agustina was too embarrassed to say what had happened, and too angry to talk to her son. Instead, she planned a long list of housekeeping chores she would make Diego perform as punishment during his five days at home. He hated helping her with housework, and always said that he would never do that type of work ever in his life.

Reluctantly, Diego silently dragged himself around the
Tonami home, helping her with the laundry and dusting,
and finding himself at the kitchen sink after every meal.

That had been one of the first times Agustina wished
Diego had a father in his life. She could have brought him
home from school and his father could have spanked him
or grounded him, she thought. Her anguish and guilt
nearly overtook her common sense, but she reminded
herself that she needed to remain calm and in control. It
wasn't Diego's fault that she'd been an unwed mother.
She knew she shouldn't take it out on him.

Agustina sat on the library couch with the old photo of
Diego resting on her knees. She studied his face for
glimpses of his father's features, which she could barely
recall because their encounter had been so brief. She
never really knew where Diego's father had come from
and certainly had no idea where he was now. He was like
a ghost in Agustina's life; if she tried to look too closely,
his image vanished in the thin air of confusion. She
longed to tell him how sorry she was that Diego had not
had him in his life. She wished she had not gotten pregnant without being married first. And she wished she had
finished school.

Agustina had been chosen to be the class valedictorian. She had outscored her classmates on all the exams. Her grades demonstrated exceptional work and she'd completed all the classes needed to be the number-one student in her class of three hundred.

Her parents were constantly congratulated for Agustina's academic record, and, while they were pleased, they were not overly impressed with grades. Agustina's standing in school was not a frequent topic of discussion at the Dominguez dinner table, because no plans for college would ever be made. In such a traditional Mexican family, the daughters never left home until they were turned over to responsible husbands. Regardless of Agustina's potential, higher education was not in the offing.

Her senior year was the best. She rode to school with friends instead of taking the bus, a change her father had surprisingly agreed to. The 1967 Ford Mustang made the girls feel like they were on top of the world. Her parents had been hesitant to grant permission, worrying that she was going to get in some kind of trouble by going to school in a car. Her parents were so strict that the only thing she could get away with was an occasional peroxide hair-coloring. Her father never commented on her dirt-blonde hair; perhaps he felt he had to make a concession somewhere. He even stuck up for her when her brothers teased her about it.

Before the Christmas break, the school held its annual winter ball. Every girl wanted to go, but in those days they had to wait to be asked. When the formal dance was only one week away, Agustina's girlfriends all had dates. She was disappointed that no boy had invited her, as this was her last chance to go. Her father hadn't allowed her to attend the dance the last three years, and word got around at school that she had very conservative parents. The boys shied away from inviting her to go anywhere. She guessed they didn't want to face her father or brothers.

Three days before the dance, Elisa, Agustina's best friend, telephoned with good news: She'd found a date for her. Agustina remembered that day clearly because it rained in the valley, a rare occurrence in the lower desert. As the dark clouds approached, Agustina and her mother had grabbed the laundry from the clotheslines strung between the tall salt cedars.

The news delighted Agustina. Elisa's brother Fred was in the military and his friend Ollie was visiting over the weekend. They were on their last leave before going to

Vietnam. Ollie would escort Agustina to the dance. She hung up the receiver and rushed back to help her mother, anxious and scared.

"Mom, can I please go to the winter dance this year?" She anticipated a negative answer, and kept her eyes on the wooden clothespins as she tossed them into a bucket.

"In this house, your father is boss," her mother responded. "If he lets you go to this dance, I can go along with it," she added. Her words were firm, and Agustina could see that her mother wanted her to go to the dance but was not sure her domineering husband would agree. Agustina could see the approval in her mother's eyes.

As she followed her mother along the clothesline she tried to convince her to help her get permission.

"But Mom," she said. "Dad won't let me go unless you talk him into it," Agustina begged. "We're all going in a group of girls. You know Elisa, Maria, and Laura," she added. She didn't tell her mother she had a date for the dance. No date was acceptable, much less an older military man. The Vietnam War was a sensitive issue with her father. Two of Agustina's brothers were in the Army but had not yet been sent overseas. The subject was never brought up for fear they would be next in line to go to Asia. Government and politics weren't discussed in their home. To other farmers who mentioned the war Roberto Dominguez always said, "Whatever Uncle Sam does is good for me. I have to work to support my family regardless."

When Agustina's mother came to her bedroom to say goodnight, she wore a mixed expression of pride and concern. As she kissed her youngest child, she whispered that she had convinced Agustina's father to allow her to go to the dance, but just for a few hours.

Agustina was ecstatic. For the last three years, everyone always talked about the dance as *the* event of the year. She immediately called Elisa to relay the green light.

• • •

ON THE NIGHT OF THE DANCE, the girls picked Agustina up in the Mustang. They were all dressed up. Agustina had never gone to so much trouble for her personal appearance. Her brothers had made fun of the enormous plastic curlers she'd worn for about twenty-four hours, but she didn't care. She thought the effort made her cheap hair-coloring look elegantly natural.

INFALLIBILITY

For the youngest in a family that had grown to nine children, buying a new dress for a one-time event was out of the question. Instead Agustina's mother allowed her to borrow a friend's fancy red skirt. The shiny satin perfectly coordinated with a light pink chiffon blouse someone had given to Altagracia. Agustina was just glad to be going at all, but she was pretty sure that she did look especially nice.

The girls had arranged to meet their dates outside a popular steakhouse. Agustina was very nervous about going to the dance with someone she didn't know. All she knew about him was that he had volunteered to go with her. She guessed that made him a nice guy. But what did he look like? Was he cute? Did he have a girlfriend? She asked herself a million questions.

The boys were waiting just outside the double doors of the restaurant. The girls giggled at the sight of them, probably more from nervousness than anything else. From the car, the guys looked like they were also laughing. Up close, Agustina could see that her date was wearing his dress uniform.

He stood straight as the girls approached. His dark green uniform was decorated with colorful strands of ribbon and shiny medals. A tiny rifle pin rested over his heart. Elisa's brother introduced him to everyone, and he extended his hand to shake Agustina's in greeting.

His handshake was firm, and he was tall and handsome. He was only twenty-two, but he definitely looked more mature than the senior boys she knew at school, partly because of his dark mustache. Agustina was not at all disappointed to be in his company. She was pleasantly impressed with his deep voice and assertive yet polite manner. Perhaps it was the uniform that immediately transformed him into a Prince Charming.

The three couples stayed at the prom for only an hour. The school chaperones understood that this was, in large part, an "in and out" function where the students dropped by mostly to get their pictures taken. Ollie and Agustina took their turn posing, and his arm around her waist made her feel important and included. When the photographer's attendant asked for their home addresses so that the pictures could be mailed later, Agustina's eyes widened with fear. What if her parents saw those photos when they arrived? Ollie seemed to know what was wrong and quickly said, "Just send them all to me." Before leaving the ballroom the couples danced to several slow songs. Agustina was in heaven as she rested her head on

Ollie's broad shoulders. The favorite song that year
seemed to be "96 Tears."

Eventually the guys persuaded their dates to go for a
drive. The girls followed along reluctantly. Though everyone knew that most couples went out to park on this
memorable night, Agustina had never imagined herself
outside under the silvery desert moon on this occasion.

Elisa's boyfriend and Ollie had prepared an aluminum
container filled with ice, beer, and wine. Agustina was surprised at the sight of liquor. The young men were pleased
with themselves at the success of their idea to have a
drink in the middle of the desert. The cool weather was
perfect and coyotes howled in the distance. Bats darted
overhead and owls hooted at the glittering stars.

They'd driven the girls to a desert ridge on Bullfrog Road.
When the cars were parked, Ollie pulled out three large
pieces of cardboard and laid them so they could all sit on
the edge of the ridge where the distant lights of Niland
twinkled in competition with the moonlight.

The boys began to drink while the girls just stared at each
other. Agustina knew that Elisa would soon begin to
drink, too. Elisa had done it before after one of the foot-

ball games. Maria and Laura did not need much prodding
to accept Budweisers from one of the guys. Ollie watched
Agustina as she stared at her friends.

Agustina had never tasted beer or wine. Her mother
always said that drinking wasn't good for anybody. But
her friends looked like they were having a lot of fun.
Agustina was struggling mentally and her friends could
see it in her face. One sip couldn't hurt, she told herself.
Everyone was encouraging her to join the group.

Ollie sat close to Agustina on the ridge, but she was pre-
occupied with keeping her borrowed clothes clean.
Eventually he placed his arm around her shoulders and
with his free hand offered her some white wine. Agustina
accepted the small paper cup. The bitter drink puckered
her lips, but she wanted to be part of the crowd and that
was that. After the wine disappeared from the cup,
Agustina had another and another until she lost count of
how many cups of the magical liquid she had consumed.
It was a painless encounter with an unfamiliar dimension,
and it seemed to make the stars shine more brightly.

She began to feel like a passenger on a tiny raft floating
down the Colorado River, light and bouncy but slightly
out of control. Her arms felt heavy, and though she could

feel her legs pressed against the cardboard she knew she could not stand up. Her feet were stretched beyond the ridge, and she dug in with her sandal heels to stop the vertigo. Soon they all were laughing and cheering at every little unimportant thing.

Although Ollie probably had nothing to cheer about, since he was leaving to fight a war in a few days, he cheered with the rest of the group and offered to throw a party on his return from Vietnam. Everyone drank a toast to his plans and pledged to attend. The liquor made everyone giddy, and they joked about school, teachers, and even their own silly laughter. Agustina was grateful that her date kept her company on the piece of cardboard.

Ollie had loosened his uniform tie and rolled up his long sleeves. Agustina had forgotten about her red satin skirt. The other couples moved off to nearby desert rocks, leaving Agustina and her date alone. The laughter and chatter continued but now it was of a more private nature.

Agustina could just about see the shadows of her girl-friends in the distance. Ollie began to rub her shoulders, and when he felt her loosen up he carefully lowered her back onto the cardboard. She welcomed the relief from her dizziness, and then he laid down beside her.

He started rubbing her thighs over her satin skirt. When she didn't object, he slowly moved his hands beneath her skirt to the edges of her panties. But she was barely aware. The wine had washed away her physical and emotional restraint. She was so high that whatever he was doing reinforced the lightness of her mind. As a matter of fact, his touches felt good to her. She hadn't realized that male hands on her buttocks could feel so good. Even his smell aroused her. It was obvious to her later that he knew exactly what he was doing, and she resented the fact that she was inexperienced. But at the time the only thing she knew for sure was that she needed to find a restroom.

Ollie helped her get up from the cardboard. Her bladder was just about to burst. There were no toilets around; Agustina would have to go right there in the desert. The problem was that she was too wobbly to squat. It would be a major disaster without help.

But Ollie knew exactly what was going on with her. He guided Agustina to a large stone only a few yards away. She figured she could hold onto the rock for support, but she was out of luck. The smooth rock provided no crevices to grab. She was so drunk that she could not balance by herself. Ollie lifted her under her armpits and told her to drop her panties. She had no choice but to do as he directed. He politely focused on the moon while he held on to her.

The ends of her fingers tingled in a funny way. She could barely find her own underwear. And, when she did, she hardly had the energy to bring them down far enough so that she could go. Years later, in Dr. Tonami's library, she learned in books about the importance of motor skills. But on this night, without Ollie's help, she would have dropped to the ground like a stone.

She urinated for what seemed a lifetime, and when she was done it took all her concentration to raise her underwear back to her hips. She could feel the thick folds of cotton stuck against her thighs. Ollie stood her against a huge rock while he turned his body to relieve himself. She could hear the urine form a single spout. Bulls on the farm made the same sound, she thought to herself, and giggled.

To her chagrin, she could not move from the rock. She knew she looked stupid. Ollie pulled her into his strong arms and carried her a short distance, then lowered her onto the cardboard. As he cradled her like a small child, she could feel his hand search for her softest parts. Like magic, her chiffon blouse fell away from her shoulders.

His lips moved quickly yet tenderly over her breasts. Her thighs parted as Ollie reached beneath her skirt and pulled her bunched-up panties back down. Her legs stretched involuntarily with an ache she had never felt before. Recovering her motor skills, she investigated his body with pleasure and amazement.

Faster than she could imagine, one soft part of the young military recruit turned into a powerful force within her own defenseless hands. He rolled her panties the rest of the way off and she locked her legs around his hips. Little did Agustina know that her body was a fertile valley like the one which physically surrounded her. It was as if water had been brought for the first time to the lower desert of California — the physical contact encouraged the bloom of eros.

The exotic combination of the cool nighttime desert and their hot desire created a perfect scene for ecstasy. But it was over as quickly as it started, and the fullness of Agustina's womanly passion departed, leaving her split into a nightmare of pathos.

Ollie stood immediately and pulled up his pants. Sheepishly, he helped her sit up, and in what seemed slow motion pulled the chiffon blouse over her bare shoulders, as if to cover the raw emotions. Little did he know that the scar of a moment already slipping away from both of them would create an infallible connection to life itself.

The cardboard was kicked into the sand where the wet spots would not be obvious in the moonlight. As they walked to the car Agustina looked back toward the cardboard as if she had left something behind. She was dumbfounded. She wanted to cry but was in shock over what she had allowed to happen under the guise of "feeling good."

"I'll write you from 'Nam," he said as he escorted her to the Mustang where her girlfriends were waiting. But Agustina's voice had disappeared in shame. And Ollie never wrote.

3

Chapter 3

By mid-February, the other girls had received their pictures from the dance. Agustina was relieved that she did not have photos to remind her of her shameful actions that night. Every evening she stared at the sky and hoped that the moon and the stars would forgive her.

Everyone at school was looking forward to spring and graduation. Agustina was scheduled to receive several awards in addition to her role as valedictorian. But the shadow of that December night hung over her like a dark cloud. She had missed her period two months in a row.

As often as she had complained about having her period, this was one time that she appreciated and looked forward to the inconvenience it caused. She knew that its absence meant something wasn't right, and she would soon have to share the problem with her mother.

Around the time she should have started bleeding in March, she began to feel different inside. Her stomach felt full and sometimes uneasy, and eventually she began to throw up everything she ate. Her favorite foods looked unappealing and sometimes smelled nasty.

Something was terribly wrong, and she was afraid. She expected her worst nightmare had come true, so she didn't say much to anyone. Every time she went to the bathroom she looked at the lining of her panties in hopes of seeing the familiar stains.

It was late April when Agustina realized she could no longer hide her condition. She was becoming slower in her actions and hungrier at dinner. Her mother had observed the growth of Agustina's breasts and thought that her daughter was developing into a woman suddenly. But as time passed she recognized the familiar symptoms of pregnancy.

One day in mid-May, a few weeks before graduation, Agustina didn't feel well. Her mother suggested she stay home from school, and then, when they were alone, delivered her precise assessment of Agustina's situation. The two women cried the entire morning. Agustina's mother cried because of what her husband would say and do.

Agustina cried because she felt she had let her mother down. One night out and she had ruined her own life. They hugged each other in desperation.

No one in the family ever forgot the night that Roberto Dominguez found out his youngest daughter was pregnant. Altagracia told her husband the bad news and did all she could to defend her daughter as a woman. Roberto alternately cried and yelled in anger and frustration. Altagracia was like a fierce lioness protecting her cub from the enemy, fearful that her child would be taken away.

Agustina and the other children weren't included in the discussion, but they could hear it from their rooms and even from outside the house where they took turns pacing as their parents fought. Agustina's mother was determined to negotiate a compromise, but no matter how hard she cried or how loudly she argued, she was not able to convince her husband to allow their daughter to remain at home under any circumstances.

Roberto had a narrow, macho view: Agustina had embarrassed the home and the family before the community and the world, and most of all she had humiliated her family before God. She would have to leave home before she brought any more grief to the family.

Agustina ran from the house in shame and, not knowing where else to go, went straight to the Tonamis' house and told them what had happened.

The Tonamis were concerned that Agustina's mistake should not be made worse by the pressure her father felt to send her away. The Japanese family still were indebted to the Mexican family for all they had done during the war. They discussed the situation with their sons, and Thomas Tonami agreed to hire Agustina in his own home as a helper for his wife and young children. Agustina's fantasies of someday attending college came to a grinding halt; as a high school dropout, her life would become devoted to her child and to her work as a maid. Despite all she had achieved, she would follow in her mother's footsteps after all, underprivileged and uneducated.

Recalling her mother's hard work as a maid brought Agustina back to the present and her own waiting chores. She rose slowly from the comfortable sofa and returned the photo of the boys to its place on the library wall. She knew she could spend the whole day thinking about things that didn't get her anywhere.

Any time Dr. Tonami was gone she seemed to take her sweet time getting her chores done, and today was no dif-

ferent than any other day in the past few months. She
moved at a leisurely pace through Dr. Tonami's bedroom,
dusting and straightening. He never really made much of
a mess but he liked everything to be orderly. Agustina
thought the only thing that needed organizing was the tie
hanger in his closet. Without his wife to help him, the
doctor had a difficult time selecting ties to match his suits.
He always pulled out about a dozen and laid them out on
the bed to study them until Agustina finally chose one for
him. After he left for work Agustina would put the others
back in the closet and then gather his dirty clothes for the
laundry.

These tasks had always been done by Maki, his wife, until
she became too sick with breast cancer to leave her bed.
Agustina missed Maki. The two had become companions
over the years, providing each other with friendship and
support, especially during times of loneliness. Photos of
Maki filled the room with fragile memories held together
in golden frames.

Now it was Agustina who left the room with Dr. Tonami's
soiled clothes in her arms. She walked downstairs to the
laundry room with a quicker step, wanting to spend as little time as possible in the sad bedroom. Being in the room
where the Tonamis had made love caused her to think of

all her mistakes in life — in particular, that one December
night that brought her to a life of servitude.

She always wondered what having a husband might have
been like. Being held close every night was something she
could only imagine. She would never know the feeling of
waking up in the arms of a strong man. She would never
have a real family. It was too late, she thought, and
menopause was just around the corner anyway.

While Dr. Tonami's clothes were in the washer, Agustina
went outside to feed the colorful fish. She loved to watch
them shoving and splashing as she tossed the pellets on
the surface of the pond. Some of the pellets fell on the
large lily plants while others disappeared instantly into
wide, waiting mouths. The bronze Wenyu danced aggres-
sively among the other fish. She thought their dramatic
tails and bright colors added to their ability to get what
they wanted out of life.

She sat on the polished rock next to the pond. It was
soothing to watch the waters turn as the fish challenged
one another for the morsels of food. When all the food
was gone, she loved to watch the water become calm
again, reflecting the clouds. The diminishing ripples
relaxed her.

Taking a long, thin stick she kept near the pond, she
stretched as far as she could to flip over the large, green
lily leaves so that the trapped pellets fell into the water. It
was as if she were treating the fish to dessert after their
meal. It was her favorite part of the feeding.

The carp reminded her of the time that Diego stole some
fish from the Tonamis' pond. He was in junior high school
then, but to Agustina it seemed like only yesterday.

Diego had found a large plastic bucket behind the greenhouse, and thought that no one saw him fill it with fish
from the pond. His skinny hands worked quickly to grab
the slippery catch. But Dr. Tonami was watching Diego
from behind a Japanese folding screen near the window.
When Diego left through the back gate on his bicycle, Dr.
Tonami followed at a distance in his car.

He intercepted the sale of his fish to one of Diego's
friends. Diego confessed that his plan had been to sell
them for money to buy cigarettes. Dr. Tonami scolded
Diego and sent him home, pretending that he would tell
Agustina although he did not until years later. But after
this incident, he began to monitor his sons' time with
Diego. He was worried about the boy's changing behavior
and rough friends.

After cigarettes came marijuana. After the pot came harder drugs, making life more difficult for everyone around Diego, including Agustina. She blamed herself for not realizing early on that her son was using drugs. He had been the nicest boy a mother could ever want, and she had no way of recognizing that he was being nice because he was high most of the time.

At first Diego got high to get away from the pressure he felt from his mother. The euphoria he felt let him be tolerant of her maternal demands. But as time passed and he used more and harder drugs to achieve that high, Diego began to care less and less what Agustina or anyone thought about what he was doing.

• • •

LIKE BRANDS FOREVER MARKING CATTLE, Agustina's memories of the bad times had scarred her permanently. Her guilt over the way Diego had come into the world grew to encompass a burden of responsibility for everything he did wrong, and for all the ways she had failed to correct his problems.

It was late October in 1985 when Agustina received a

midnight call from the police department. Diego had gone to a football game earlier in the evening but had not returned home. She'd been up pacing the floor in the small kitchen, waiting for him. The desk officer told her that Diego had been caught smoking pot with some older boys. Although he was only fifteen, he was arrested and taken to the lockup. Her heart dropped to her feet when the officer described the possible legal consequences. Agustina rushed out of the house and headed angrily to the police station, borrowing Maki's car.

She had to identify herself to several levels of officers before she was allowed to speak to the sergeant in charge of her son's case. Agustina argued fervently that her son would no longer be allowed to run with the same crowd. It was obvious to her that the officer did not believe a word she said, but more serious cases awaited his attention. Diego was released to her custody. "Next time," she was warned, "you will have to visit him in juvenile hall."

Agustina had nothing to say to Diego on the way home, and had cried all her available tears in front of the police. Diego showed no remorse, which made Agustina wonder if she was wrong to defend him. But she felt sorry for him because he didn't have a father at home to help him grow up the right way.

Remembering that night, Agustina still wondered if having a husband, a father for Diego, would have made a difference. She had always been so strong-willed, thinking that she could handle whatever was thrown at her. She felt stupid for not having used that strength to protect him from his self-destruction.

Instead, she had often prayed to the Virgin of Guadalupe to help her with Diego. She asked the Virgin to guide him in the company of his friends, and to protect him from bad people. But it all seemed so futile. Everything that happened seemed the opposite of her prayers.

Agustina could see now that she had been blind to the problems Diego faced. Because she had been protected from nearly everything in her own youth, she assumed she could do the same for her son. And like most parents, she denied the possibility that her child was really caught up in the wrong things. She believed that any problems could be addressed by a sternly delivered lecture at home.

Even Dr. Tonami had seen the dangerous path Diego was on. Agustina didn't know at the time that Dr. Tonami purposefully kept his sons away from hers. By junior high school, the distance between Diego and the Tonami boys was obvious, but Agustina believed that cultural differences were the cause. Now, looking back, she realized that Dr. Tonami's loyalty to his family's friendship with hers had kept him from criticizing her or from asking her to take Diego and move away.

After marijuana came the white powder. By the time Diego was eighteen, his cocaine habit could be supported only by theft. He was cagey and manipulative, and his ability to work with his hands and his mind led him to steal cars. In an old garage on the outskirts of Los Angeles, Diego and other young addicts swapped parts and created almost-new vehicles for sale on the black market. The same group of men who had first sold him cocaine kept him working like a slave to earn enough money to meet his increasingly demanding habit.

Of course, Diego never told Agustina any of this. She got a clue when a policeman visited her at home one day to question her about stolen car parts. When she asked Diego about it, he told her it must have been a mistake. She guessed that he was probably in trouble but she didn't want to acknowledge how boundless the problems were. She knew that he loved her in his own way and tried to protect her from his life.

Eventually, though, Diego became mean to her and to everyone around him. He lost his childhood friends. Agustina thought he resembled an angry animal, lashing out violently without concern for the harm he caused himself. Many times he woke up in the morning with bruises and cuts but could never remember when or where they had happened.

On his worst days, he challenged and threatened Agustina, telling her that she was a nobody. He raged at her for allowing him to be born a bastard. He swore she had ruined his life. His words cut Agustina to the quick but she was afraid to say anything for fear it would make him angrier. She was also afraid that Dr. Tonami would ask them to leave. But Diego was not at home much, so she could swallow her distress and continue to serve the Tonami family. She kept the doors locked all the time just in case Diego came home during the day. She no longer wanted him in the Tonamis' home for fear that he would steal something.

On New Year's Day in 1993 Agustina realized that Diego had stolen all of the savings she had stashed away in the house. He had learned her secret codes and defied the security systems she used. But she was afraid to say anything to him because she was scared for her own safety.

INFALLIBILITY

Late in the day Diego came home high and sick. As he stumbled through the kitchen, he coughed up blood on the clean linoleum floor. Agustina instinctively rushed to help him. Her maternal concern was met with a fist in her face and a kick below her knees that knocked her to the floor.

She could feel the warm blood draining from her mouth onto her arm, where her head rested uneasily. The room seemed to turn in slow motion. She wished she could stop the turning and make it go in reverse, make the entire scene go away, take her love back and not receive his hatred. Her body ached and she couldn't raise herself from the floor. Diego's labored breathing from the couch told her he had passed out.

Slowly, she rolled over on her knees. The pain where her son had kicked her on the ankle nearly made her cry out, but she clenched her teeth and crawled the short distance to the phone. She dialed the only number she knew by heart: Dr. Tonami's. She did not know what to say other than that she was hurt.

Dr. Tonami was out of his house and across the yard to the guesthouse within minutes, using his own key to unlock the door. As a coroner accustomed to reviewing murder scenes, he knew immediately what had happened by taking a quick look around the tiny house. He pulled ice from the freezer and twisted the cubes from the pink rubber trays into a kitchen towel. He gave the ice pack to Agustina to hold against her cheek. He said nothing as tears rolled sadly down her red, swollen face, but handed her a moistened paper towel to wipe the blood from her mouth.

Agustina tried to get up from the floor but could not put weight on her feet. Dr. Tonami looked at her ankle. Diego had aimed a perfect hit on the inside of the bone, causing a major fracture. Dr. Tonami rushed back to his home and returned with more ice. He carefully put his arms beneath Agustina's and helped to pull her up while she lifted her body with the strength of her unbreakable spirit. She held onto his shoulder and hopped on one foot to her bed.

Dr. Tonami worked quietly, elevating her leg on several pillows and fitting the cold towel filled with ice over her swelling ankle.

"You have a broken ankle, Agustina," he said matter-of-factly. "I need to drive you to the hospital for X-rays."

Agustina did not want to go to the hospital. She knew

there would be questions about how her injuries had happened. It was too embarrassing. She begged Dr. Tonami not to take her to the hospital, and promised him she would heal soon. Dr. Tonami's dark eyes filled with tears.

Her own tears kept coming, from humiliation and from pain. She could not understand why things had turned out this way. From her bed she stared accusingly at the Virgin of Guadalupe. She felt guilty for blaming the Virgin but needed someone to help her carry this pain. What had she done to deserve this? She silently questioned the statue while Dr. Tonami fussed around her. He brought her a glass of water and two pills, which she assumed were aspirin and swallowed gratefully. Within twenty minutes, she was sleeping peacefully.

When she woke up, Agustina was lying in a hospital bed. A large, white plaster cast had been molded around her lower right leg. Dr. Tonami was there, watching her every move like a mother hen. She reached toward her face where it hurt but her right arm had a small needle taped into it, so she let it fall back to her side. By the side of the bed a metal stand held a plastic bag that dripped its clear contents down a tube and into a vein.

"I need to get out of here," she told Dr. Tonami in a small

but panic-stricken voice. "I don't want to talk to the police about this." Dr. Tonami saw the distress on her face and leaned over to pat her on the shoulder.

"We are in a doctor's office, Agustina, not in the hospital. You won't have to speak to anyone about what happened," he told her. Agustina was profoundly embarrassed. *Thank the Virgen de Guadalupe for Dr. Tonami*, she repeated silently to herself. She was forever thankful to him for so many things, she thought. His family had always taken care of hers, and he had accepted her into his home when her father rejected her. She did not know who else to turn to for help. Her eyelids slowly closed, and she prayed she would not wake up again into her miserable reality.

For the next five weeks, Agustina hopped and limped through her chores and tried to forget the incident that brought so much pain to her heart. When it was time for her cast to come off, Dr. Tonami kindly brought the doctor to the house to prevent her any embarrassment. In the meantime, Diego had disappeared, unaware — or perhaps unconcerned — that he was the monster responsible for his mother's injuries.

Agustina's final episode of defeat came at the end of that
year. Other homes were dressed for the holidays in their
finest glittering attire, but the Tonami home was
unadorned. Without his wife to enjoy the festivities, Dr.
Tonami planned a trip with his sons to visit relatives in
Japan instead. Agustina decided to try to mend her relationship with her parents, and called to ask if she and
Diego could spend the holidays in Imperial County. For
the first time in many years, her entire family was gathering at her brother's home in Niland, and her parents were
thrilled at the chance to heal the old wounds.

4

Chapter 4

Diego showed up late in the afternoon the day
before Christmas Eve. Agustina was trying hard
to be nice to him so that he would cooperate
with her during the trip to visit her family.

As he walked into the kitchen she could smell the sweet,
woody aroma of marijuana. His eyes were glassy and his
mouth was set in a tight frown. Agustina always handled
him the same way when she knew he was high: She
offered him something to eat. He would wolf down whatever she made for him and then fall asleep. But this time,
he didn't answer her. He walked to the stove and took the
pan of beans from the burner and threw it at her. She
ducked and the pan flew over her head, the *frijoles* splattering in every direction. She screamed at him to stop, but
something told her he couldn't hear her.

He was grabbing all the pans and skillets and throwing

them at the walls. With each lob he yelled obscenities about Agustina and her family. Then he raised one of the old kitchen chairs above his head and smashed it over the table into a hundred pieces. Agustina was beside herself with fear and anger. She cried at him to stop being ridiculous. Diego leaned for a moment against the kitchen counter with his back to her, his chest heaving from exertion. When he turned to face her, he held a carving knife that she had left at the side of the sink. His eyes were filled with rage and the veins in his neck bulged. When she reached to grab the knife from him, the sharp point caught the soft flesh of her hand between the thumb and forefinger. Diego called her vile names she had never heard before, berating her for being stupid.

She moved toward the back door. The slow motion of her nightmares had returned, and she fumbled with the latch before it finally opened and she ran into the yard, crying for help. She cried out loud to the Virgin for a miracle.

Diego grabbed her right arm as if he had forgotten Agustina was his mother. He pinned her arm tightly behind her back and pointed the knife at her stomach, forcing her fear into shock. Dr. Tonami was already gone to Japan, but she cried desperately for help and hoped that someone could hear her pleas. The knife blade

flashed in front of her pounding heart, and her legs gave
way as she passed out from the pain and fear.

She was not surprised to wake up in a hospital that time.
Her body was covered with bruises and blood seeped
through the heavy bandage on her upper arm. The last
thing she remembered before blacking out was the image
of her patron, the Virgin of Guadalupe.

When a nurse came in to check on her, Agustina asked
what had happened and how she had gotten to the hospital. The nurse looked at her chart and told her that someone had called 911 seeking help. "A detective was here
earlier this morning," the nurse added. "He said they
found you outside your house last night. He'll be back in
a little while to take a report from you before you go
home," she said before she left the room.

Agustina wished Dr. Tonami was not out of the country.
He could tell her what to say to the detective. What was
she going to do now? *Virgencita de Guadalupe, please help
me out of this mess*, she prayed.

But her first visitor, much to her chagrin, was Diego. She
felt as cold as a winter night in the Arctic. He said he was
there to take her home, and she burst into tears.

Diego sat on the chair next to the bed while the nurse
gathered Agustina's few belongings. He held her hand tenderly and acted as if he didn't know anything about what
had happened. She was confused, wanting to reject his
love but not knowing how to reject the love of her own
child. She was angry about the pain he had caused her,
and embarrassed about whoever it was who had called
911. She knew Diego hadn't made that call; he would
rather have seen her die.

When the detective walked in, Diego's hand stiffened
around Agustina's. She felt stupid; she should have
known better. Of course Diego knew what had happened.
He was probably only there to make sure she didn't tell
on him. She could see it in her son's eyes — deep, dark,
and vacant. He could care less how she was doing.

The detective questioned Agustina, and Diego answered
for her. He said that he had found a note in the kitchen
that said his mother had been taken to the hospital. As he
spoke he held Agustina's left hand in a loving manner.
When the detective asked questions about her injuries,
Agustina felt her son's grip tighten.

"I really don't know how this whole thing happened," she
told the detective. "I was approached from the back."

"What about that big cut on your right hand?"

"That must have happened when I fell to the ground," she lied.

Her son was satisfied, and loosened his grip on her hand. Diego reminded Agustina of a snake that has patiently swallowed a large meal. He was content, and yet, like a killer snake, had enough venom left to stiffen her body on the spot.

The detective pulled out a business card and handed it to Diego. "Call me if anything else comes to mind that you think I should know," he said. "And take good care of your mother." He gave Diego a long look, and then left them alone.

Agustina guessed that hers was not a high-priority case for the police department. The news every night showed real emergencies — murders, shootings, and rapes. Her problems were far too minor to get much attention.

Diego drove her home in silence. She didn't say a word, acting as if she was too sick to speak. She was disgusted with herself for having lied to protect her son. She felt ugly and terrorized. The doctor had prescribed morphine, and she was grateful for the way it let her forget both the surface pain and the deep hurt.

She had hidden the pills in her skirt pocket so that Diego would not know about them, and she looked forward to taking twice the prescribed dose as soon as she got home, so that she could go to sleep and not have to deal with him. She was emotionally drained, and hoped two pills would relax her to the point of ignorance about her surroundings.

The first thing she saw as they walked through the back door was *frijoles* scattered into a million particles. The cold smell of dried beans was too familiar. Cleaning would have to wait as Agustina was in no condition to do housework.

Diego actually helped her to her bed before he left. After she heard the door close behind him, she called her family and told them she had fallen outside in the garden and would not be able to make the trip this time. Then she eagerly took her pills and felt much better almost immediately. Within minutes she was sleeping deeply.

When she awoke, Diego was gone. Her first thought was to kneel before the Virgin of Guadalupe and pray for help. "Please help my son," she begged aloud as she struggled to sit up. Her body was sore and her mouth was dry from the morphine, but her spirit was unbreakable. "Please keep him safe from danger. And please, give me the answer to this problem before me." Agustina prayed so passionately that tears emerged at the edges of her eyes.

She forced her weak body upright and stretched to pull her rosary from the bedpost. What else was there to do but pray that the evil would leave her son? Again she wished she had had a husband who could have disciplined Diego a little more before he became a threat to her. It was her fault that Diego was fatherless — or was it? For the first time it occurred to her that Ollie might have made it through the Vietnam War and just never bothered to get in touch with her. She had anxiously watched the nightly news until Diego was born, hoping for a glimpse of her baby's father. When Elisa's brother Alfredo was killed in a Vietcong attack, Agustina assumed that Ollie had died too. She erased him from her mind and concentrated on her son.

Diego was resentful of not having a father and had made his resentment known in many ways. Agustina felt that through her son, life was teaching her a lesson about deception as punishment for what she had done to her parents by getting pregnant.

• • •

RELIVING DIEGO'S WORST DAYS caused Agustina's palms to sweat. Every time she dwelled on the past, her sticky hands would shake her thoughts back to reality.

Agustina calmly wiped her hands against her hips as she stood up from her seat on the pond's edge. *Thank God Dr. Tonami is out of town,* she thought. *I've been too slow today.* As she walked back inside to move the clothes from the washer to the dryer, she heard the phone ringing. She hurried to the kitchen to answer it. A familiar voice was on the other end.

"Hello, Doctor." Agustina was surprised since he rarely called during a workday. Dr. Tonami politely informed her that he would be arriving in time for dinner the following night, and would be bringing an overnight guest. Agustina always appreciated Dr. Tonami's formal way of letting her know that company was coming. It gave her time to prepare something special. Dr. Tonami's wife had been very good as a hostess, and now he depended on Agustina to take care of all the arrangements for the guests.

Dr. Tonami was bringing home a detective from Ventura County. Agustina guessed that the case they were working

on must be more complicated than Dr. Tonami had anticipated. She had seen a news report about it, a gruesome
murder of a young woman. Dr. Tonami had been called in
to provide a second autopsy on the mutilated corpse.
Agustina could not imagine how he could tolerate such
horrid scenes and cold bodies.

Poor woman, she thought as she walked back to the laundry room. *She really got treated horribly in her final hours.*
Agustina was curious about the events that led to the
young woman's death. *Was her killer someone she loved?*
As usual, her mind jumped to thoughts of Diego. She
remembered the time a policeman appeared at the door
one sunny afternoon, looking for her son. Diego had hidden just out of sight with a pair of scissors pointed into
the soft flesh of his mother's waist while Agustina
answered questions through the screen door.

As soon as the officer left, Agustina knelt again before the
blessed Virgin and cried her heart out. She did not know
what else to do. Agustina felt she did not have the right to
run to anyone for help because she was responsible for
Diego. Besides, everyone she knew had already helped
her in many ways. "*Virgencita de Guadalupe*, please show
me the way to help my son," she prayed. "Please enlight-
en him so that he no longer hurts people or steals from

them. I pray to you for your humble and wise assistance and your guidance. I give myself to you as you guide me. My heart and soul are yours, my blessed Lady."

Agustina dedicated so much energy to prayer that on some days, like this one, she fell asleep in front of the statue. It was during one of those exhausted naps that she had a new vision for life. In a dream the Virgin asked Agustina to take Diego to Mexico to visit her shrine. Agustina's mother had often spoken of her own visit to the shrine, but Agustina had not thought to go there herself. She was deeply touched by the dream because it felt so real. It also reminded her that she had named Diego after the Indian peasant boy who was blessed by an appearance of the Virgin.

In Agustina's dream the blessed woman welcomed them to her huge shrine in Mexico City. For many days, the dream was kept alive by Agustina's belief that the Virgin had given her a direction that needed to be followed. But Agustina also liked the idea of visiting the shrine as another way to seek help. Besides, in Mexico City she would be just a few hours away from the town where her parents had retired. Perhaps this time her plans to see them would not be thwarted.

For weeks, Agustina could not file the dream away. The image of the shrine kept her awake at night while it ran like an old film played over and over again. Each day she awoke as if the dream were new. Agustina tried hard to make sense of it, to interpret it another way. But it was plain and simple: Take Diego to Mexico City.

After so many years of working with the Tonami family, Agustina knew that she could take time off for a three-day vacation to visit her parents. The challenge would be to convince Diego to travel with her.

After much pleading, she was able to insure his cooperation in exchange for cash. Although she was ashamed to pay him to accompany her to Mexico after he had stolen all of her savings already, she felt it was the right thing to do. She would save again until autumn, and her hard-earned money would honor the Virgin by coercing Diego to visit his relatives.

• • •

DIEGO AND AGUSTINA ARRIVED IN MEXICO at the beginning of the rainy season in the small village of La Flor where her parents were born and now lived again.

La Flor was a tiny enclave nestled against a tall mountain. Agustina's parents sought the country air after her father retired from the Tonami ranch, and now they lived comfortably on their Social Security benefits earned in the United States. The same adobe house that had once been temporary quarters for the Tonami family during World War II was now home to the aging Dominguez couple.

The humble Mexican-style house was full of the Tonamis' Japanese touches. In the living room, old photos of Dominguez generations past decorated the walls side-by-side with small painted pictures of Japanese gardens and flowers. In the open doorway between the kitchen and the family room a short blue-and-white curtain still hung, reaching barely a third of the way down. The Dominguez family had to lower their heads to avoid the curtain as they made their way into or out of the kitchen, but their bond with the Tonami family was so strong that the curtain was a friendly reminder of that special relationship.

By the time mother and son ducked through that doorway, Diego was restless and angry. He greeted his grandparents with stiff hugs and no smile. After the brief and uncomfortable encounter, he hurried from the house and up the road to the small family-owned village stores to drink. Agustina wearily anticipated the pattern of his behavior during the short trip. She was already disappointed in his lack of respect for her parents and for the family customs of a small village. But she was the one who had bribed him to come to Mexico, so her confidence rested in the Virgin of Guadalupe. Agustina believed that a visit to the shrine would make all the difference in the world.

Despite their grandson's attitude, Agustina's parents were happy and excited to see their youngest daughter. Roberto Dominguez had reached a point in life where he could discuss the tremendous guilt he felt for having sent her away from the family, and both parents felt that they shared part of the responsibility for Diego's problems.

Even so, they were unaware of the deep trouble Diego had caused his mother. Agustina had hidden from them the hospital trips and visits from police detectives. Nevertheless, her parents wondered if Diego would have turned out better if they had allowed Agustina to remain at home.

When Diego disappeared into the village, Agustina knew he would meet other young men and drink until someone more sober dragged him home. She had cautiously reminded him about being on his best behavior in exchange for the money, but she braced herself for trouble. The trip to the shrine could not come soon enough.

• • •

DIEGO AWOKE VERY LATE the next morning and demanded breakfast. Agustina's parents were shocked by his foul mood but pretended not to notice. Hoping to keep him quiet, Agustina quickly fixed Diego some eggs and beans. He ate like a hungry animal, scooping the food into his mouth with hot tortillas. After he finished, he disappeared from the house again. Agustina fretted about her son's whereabouts, wondering how fast he could spend her five hundred dollars on Mexican beer, tequila, and marijuana.

The next day was the same. Diego slept late. Agustina peeked into the tiny room where he slept, and the smell of stale beer stung her nostrils. She had heard him come in at three in the morning, stumbling in the dark through the unfamiliar adobe house. Watching him now as he snored heavily, she could see that he was still drunk. Nevertheless, she knew that as soon as he did wake up, he'd be hungry again and demanding to be fed. No matter what he had polluted himself with the night before, he always had a great appetite the next morning.

With time to enjoy herself before Diego awoke, Agustina decided to take a walk in the hills surrounding the village. Her father reminded her that since it was the rainy season, mushrooms were popping up all over the green countryside. Agustina and her mother grabbed two plastic pails and headed toward the hills, walking and talking with many other villagers eager to hunt mushrooms.

The delightful goddess of dawn filled the blue skies with streaks of sunlight as drops of dew glistened on the grass. Mushrooms were everywhere. Agustina's mother was very particular about which ones should be picked, reminding her daughter not to touch the ones with pink undersides. The hills were covered with people, young and old, gathering the delicacies for a traditional breakfast.

Agustina's bucket was nearly filled with the delicate white fungi. The skinny stems were covered with moist dirt. She and her mother would have to clean them well before cooking them.

There were other mushrooms growing on dung and in rock crevices that looked as tasty if not better than the ones in her bucket. Out of curiosity, Agustina picked one of the skinny mushrooms growing to one side of an almost-dry cow patty. She examined it closely to see if it looked poisonous. On the soft, leathery-looking umbrella cap she noticed a tiny outline that took her breath away. There on the mushroom was a vague design resembling the Virgin of Guadalupe's head. Agustina stared in amazement at the image of her spiritual companion, then realized her mother or the other mushroom hunters might be watching. She quickly tucked the mushroom in the pocket of her jeans so that she could inspect it more closely when she was alone.

Agustina's mother was as glad for the time to visit with her daughter as she was proud of their brimming buckets of mushrooms. She had felt guilty ever since the day Agustina was sent away from home, and she knew her daughter had suffered much in the last twenty-seven years. She remembered when Agustina called her from the Tonamis' kitchen to tell her that her water had broken while she was washing dishes. Mrs. Tonami drove Agustina to General Hospital and stayed with her because Roberto Dominguez stubbornly refused to let his wife go. Altagracia was sad that she could not be with her daughter during the natural but painful event. It was she who suggested that Agustina offer her suffering to the Virgin of Guadalupe, and she who suggested that the baby be named Diego after the humble Indian boy to whom the

Virgin had appeared. Had it been a girl, Agustina would have named her Lupita, short for Guadalupe.

As he aged, her father had gradually softened his attitude toward Agustina and even offered a few apologetic words to her by phone a time or two. But mother and daughter did not have to say much to each other to know that they had both paid a terrible price for Agustina's mistake.

The women arrived home with the mushrooms just as Mr. Dominguez returned from the village store with some pork. Agustina spontaneously volunteered to cook breakfast for the family, and her tired mother was glad to sit and watch her.

As Agustina moved about the small kitchen her father stared at her with pride. He knew that she loved him despite the part of her youth he had denied her. The aroma of the frying pork and the earthy mushrooms delighted him as well. When she brought the hot tortillas to the table, the three sat down to a mouth-watering feast.

Agustina figured she would have to cook again for Diego when he decided to get out of bed. She'd thought about waking him for the special meal but decided against it in case he reacted badly. They'd be leaving tomorrow, and so far Diego had not caused any really terrible scenes in front of his grandparents.

He finally rose from his wasted night about two hours later. His hair was stiff and pointing straight out from the sides of his head where he had tossed and turned in his drunken delirium. Without greeting anyone, he rudely demanded breakfast. His grandparents watched in sorrow.

Agustina immediately acknowledged that his breakfast was in the works in hopes that he would just keep quiet. Diego had no business treating her like a maid in front of her own parents, but in the last few years she had stopped expecting anything better from him. She also knew that he could be far worse. She bottled up her anger and embarrassment and began to add wood to the fire. She missed the easy on-and-off gas stove she had been cooking on for so many years, and knew her father was too old-fashioned and stubborn to purchase a modern stove for her mother. But soon the flames would be forceful enough to burn away her frustrations and cook the pork and mushrooms for Diego.

As she waited for the fire to get hot, Agustina stood with her hands in her pockets and her head down. Her parents were silent, not wanting to say the wrong thing in front of

Diego. They were beginning to sense the discomfort between mother and son, and could tell that Diego had been drinking or something worse. He looked trashy and distant.

In her left pocket Agustina felt the smooth mushroom she had hidden there, and remembered the special outline on it. She hurried to wash it with the others soaking in a clay pot in the sink. The design was gone; the mushroom from her pocket looked no different from the rest. Her eyes must have played tricks on her, she thought. She looked again in hopes of seeing the same outline of the Virgin of Guadalupe, and for a brief instant glimpsed the image once more. This was the Virgin she had prayed to and beseeched for help.

Agustina's father startled her from behind. He took the mushroom from her and stared at it as if he hoped to see something else, too. Then with a shrug, he tossed the mushroom into the pot with the others, and thanked his daughter for the delicious breakfast.

Agustina chopped all the mushrooms together and began to fry them in lard over the flames. She added onions and garlic into the pot, and then tossed in small pieces of pork left over from the earlier meal. When the mixture was ready to eat, she added the traditional flavorings of cumin and salt, then poured the pot's contents on a huge clay plate, to which she added beans and rice as well. She slid the steaming tray in front of Diego.

Immediately, Diego took a hot tortilla and filled small pieces with the pork and mushroom combination.

"This is an excellent dish, Mother," he said between bites. His few words astonished everyone as he had said very little since arriving. Agustina was even more amazed that his words were complimentary. She smiled proudly at her parents.

As Diego ate, Agustina looked devotedly at the small statue of the Virgin of Guadalupe stationed on a corner shelf in the kitchen. She believed that the Virgin had sent her some good signs, and she silently prayed that her son would shape up. Diego cleaned his plate and looked restored from the good food.

Agustina stood from the table to clear his dishes. Diego took off for town immediately when she reminded him that they would be leaving early in the morning to visit the holy shrine of the Virgin of Guadalupe on their way back home.

Agustina and her mother walked together to the small private shrine between the kitchen and the bedrooms. As in
most Mexican houses, the altar was a place of importance
in the home. An adobe shelf held several statutes of the
Virgin of Guadalupe and other saints. Lighted candles
surrounded the Virgin. Indian-made flowers with glitter on
the petal tips surrounded the statue like a shawl. Colorful
tissue paper garlands hung over the shrine. Many of the
decorations had been there for decades and showed fly
spots. Agustina and her mother prayed the rosary with
deep devotion. They did not have to speak about their
concern for Diego, but meditated quietly together with
affection and respect.

5

Chapter 5

It was long after midnight when Agustina heard noise at the front door of her parents' home. As usual, someone had helped Diego home again. She could hear other young men outside joking about his drunkenness. The sound of boots scraping on the floor made her think they were dragging Diego into the house. When the door closed, the house got quiet again. The only sounds were from distant coyotes howling at the silver moon. Agustina's eyes closed, but a shadow of worry slept with her the rest of the night.

Menudo was waiting with hot tortillas for Agustina when she arose the next morning. The delicious beef soup was always eaten on Sundays and festive mornings. Patiently, Agustina waited an hour before knocking on the weathered, wooden bedroom door to wake Diego. She was grateful that someone in the village had brought her son back to his grandparents' house. Otherwise, she would be searching for him herself now. She called through the door that it was time to depart for home.

Then she sat down to chat with her parents in the kitchen. Out of the corner of one eye she kept a watch on Diego's bedroom door. She wanted to make sure he had time to eat his usual hearty breakfast before they left, as the bus trip to the shrine would take five hours.

An hour passed and Diego did not emerge. Agustina returned to the door, harried and impatient. She knocked first but then entered the room. Diego was lying on his stomach sideways on the bed, his long arms on the floor and his head sagging off the edge. His hair was frozen in a crazy frenzy, and he still had his clothes and shoes on. Near his head was vomit covered with gnats and flies. Agustina shook her head in disgust. Her lips curled from the sour smell as she shook him by the shoulders and told him to get up. In an instant, she realized he was not responding. She seemed to be pounding a thick block of rancid meat.

The odor of spoiled beer and rotten eggs nearly overcame her as she put her head against Diego's back to listen for a heartbeat. His body was cold. She yelled his name and shook his shoulders again, but to no avail. Her skin filled with goose bumps and her yells turned to cries of pain. Diego was dead, gone from her forever.

Agustina's parents rushed into the room to find her cradling Diego's head and rocking back forth as if he were still a tiny baby. The slimy vomit on the floor contained more life than the body of Diego. Agustina was in shock; her loud cries punctured the putrid air without consolation.

Her parents held on to her and cried in terror and guilt. Agustina clutched Diego's head next to her breast, the tears running down her face and into his hair.

Finally, Agustina's father tenderly pulled Diego from her and carefully lifted him onto his back. His face was covered with mushy particles of regurgitated food. Agustina's father rushed to get a wet towel and began to clean his grandson's once-handsome face. Her mother began to straighten up the smelly room. Some quick cleaning would need to be done before they summoned the local midwife for assistance.

When she arrived, the midwife went immediately to Diego's bedside. The elderly woman welcomed all the newborn children and bid farewell to the very sick and the dead. With wrinkled hands she motioned Agustina to leave the room while she prepared the body in the manner expected of her in the isolated Mexican village. She examined the body as she examined all bodies; she was not trained to do a formal autopsy. The ritual visit and preparation were sufficient. The midwife shook her head as she viewed Diego. She opened his mouth and looked into his ears. Then she took off his damp shirt to examine his torso.

Taking tiny green leaves from a gunny-sack pouch, she crushed the herbs and placed small amounts in each of Diego's nostrils. She then stuffed pieces of a natural cotton-like plant to hold the leaves in. Two more pieces of the cottony material went in his ears. Then she dipped mint leaves in a dish of holy water and placed them on his eyes. When she was finished, she made the sign of the cross and left the room.

Diego's grandparents immediately placed four large yellow candles around the bed to serve as religious guards of his body. Agustina's father lit the candles and the room took on an eerie quality.

Agustina was beside herself. Her sobs filled the house.

INFALLIBILITY

The last thing she expected was to return to Mexico to bury her son. With tearful eyes she looked to the Virgin of Guadalupe for answers.

Her parents led her gently from the altar back to the room where Diego was laid out in fresh clothing on the same bed where she had found him lifeless. Agustina rushed to hold him in her arms like she had when he was just an little boy. Deep down, Agustina wanted to die too. Her son had left the world without much of a fight. That was not like him. Her parents cried with her as they huddled around the young body.

Staring at her son, Agustina felt such guilt and deep regret that she fainted. When they revived her, her parents carefully explained to her the details of the midwife's examination. Diego had drowned in his own vomit, she had told them. He was sick from drinking too much beer and tequila, and was too drunk to raise his head. His lungs were filled with fluid, the midwife said.

As much pain as Diego had caused her, Agustina still loved him and could feel the maternal tugs of labor ringing with force as she rocked her son one last time. The mean soul in him had escaped his body. Her mother brought Agustina a cup of special tea made with medicinal leaves to calm her so that they could prepare for the funeral. As she relaxed she realized that she would be alone forever. She wished she could have spoken to Diego one last time about the cruelty he showed her, and she wished she had fought back for those things he had done to her. Recalling his threats and his anger when she tried to be nice to him just brought more tears to her eyes.

Their trip to the shrine of the Virgin of Guadalupe would not take place now. Instead, she prayed to the Virgin for Diego's safe journey to heaven. With all he had done wrong, she was worried that hell awaited him. She had often warned him that he would wind up in hell for all the bad things he did. Now she felt guilty for having said it.

Agustina finally realized that Diego would have to be buried in Mexico. Like villagers who passed away, Diego's body would be set out for an evening vigil and buried the next day after mass. The lack of fancy mortuaries with updated equipment and freezers dictated the schedule for Diego's final farewell. The young man would be mourned for nine days after burial. The ritual would include nine rosaries to help Diego's soul reach its eternal resting place.

By early afternoon, Diego's body lay in a simple wooden

casket. The four large candles still stood at guard by each corner. Many of the villagers came to see the body of a young man from America who died in his own vomit. Such rural people could not imagine the real life of Diego Dominguez.

Mourners gathered in the Dominguez home to pay their respects to the family. The kitchen was filled with tequila bottles, bread, sweet tamales, rice, beans, tortillas, and numerous round cheeses. This was the way of the village, the way the poor paid their condolences.

All night long, families arrived in droves to view the body. Agustina was accompanied each time to the casket by many women dressed in the dark clothes of mourning. For the first time in over a decade Diego's body rested peacefully as the visitors wondered how a man could drown on dry land.

Early the next morning, Agustina was surprised by the arrival of Dr. Tonami. She was shocked yet relieved to know that someone had called him on her behalf. She held on to him as her tears silently wetted the blue shirt she had ironed so many times for him. The normally reserved doctor hugged her and gently rubbed the back of her head.

Agustina's parents were honored that Dr. Tonami was there. They had not seen him since they moved from the Imperial Valley. Dr. Tonami greeted them warmly but immediately asked to see Diego's body. The villagers were shocked at his directness. They remembered him as a young boy who had lived in the village but had no idea that he was now a respected pathologist from a big city.

Agustina knew that her boss meant well. He had always been a kind gentleman. He cared for them and wanted to make sure she knew it. He was probably the only other individual besides Agustina who knew the tormented life Diego lived and the problems that he had caused his mother.

While the mourners gathered at the church, Dr. Tonami spent an hour with Diego's body, examining it while Agustina's father looked on. The doctor unbuttoned Diego's shirt and raised his body to examine his back, then carefully buttoned it up again. Next he unbuckled Diego's belt and lowered his trousers to examine his extremities. Dr. Tonami was thorough in his brief inspection. With much attention to detail, he returned every strand of hair and piece of clothing to the way they were before he began the examination.

Roberto Dominguez related the midwife's conclusion to
Dr. Tonami, who listened carefully to every word. Then he
pulled a zippered plastic bag from his pocket and placed
inside it a few strands of Diego's hair. With a hypodermic
syringe he drew some blood from the corpse and put it in
a small vial. The meticulous doctor then carefully
removed the cotton and leaf wads from Diego's ears and
nose. With a sharp instrument he took samples from the
cavities and placed them in a little polystyrene container.
Then he replaced the stuffing, putting the herbs in first
and then the cotton. When he was finished, he turned his
plastic gloves inside out and stuffed those in his pockets,
too. He said nothing of his findings, but left the room to
sit at Agustina's side at the church.

After the Catholic mass Diego was taken to the village
cemetery for his final resting place. At the gravesite,
Agustina knelt in front of the wooden casket. Again she
offered her son to the protection of the Virgin of
Guadalupe. She knew that her patron saint would watch
over him. Her father helped her to stand and toss a handful of red dirt over the casket. Her tears fell on the freshly
dug earth.

After the burial, Dr. Tonami said his farewells and

returned home to California. Agustina remained in Mexico. For nine days, Agustina questioned her son's life and death. She could not remember a time in her life when she was not worried about him. Each night, the rosary was attended by many women dressed in dark clothes and shawls. With them, it was difficult for Agustina to keep her emotions to herself. She wanted to tell someone about the pain Diego had caused her, but that would not have been right. The others presumed that Diego had been a good young man. She did not want to speak ill of the dead.

When the official mourning period had passed, Agustina returned to her position as housekeeper for Dr. Tonami. She was pleasantly surprised by a new coat of paint on her guesthouse, inside and out. In addition, there was new carpet over the old linoleum floor, and a new stove and refrigerator. Agustina understood that Dr. Tonami had done this for her. He wanted to cheer her after such a painful loss. Besides, the remodeling was needed after all the holes Diego had punched in the walls.

6

Chapter 6

The alarm went off at the usual time, and Agustina's eyes opened to the beautiful sight of the Virgin of Guadalupe statue on her night stand. Agustina always thought that the smile on the Virgin's face was meant for her when she first woke up. This day she sat up quickly when she remembered that Dr. Tonami was bringing a guest, for dinner. The men would be arriving at three or so and she needed extra time to prepare a good dinner.

She hurried through her morning shower and chores in her own home before rushing to the main house. She dusted the library first as it was the room where the men would talk before dinner, and then cleaned the guest bedroom. As three o'clock arrived, Agustina was all set to welcome Dr. Tonami and his guest. She had even prepared a platter of fresh fruit and vegetable slices for them to snack on.

Agustina hurried to prepare ingredients for the evening meal. She knew she should pinch herself whenever her mind started to dwell on Diego. She had wasted much time analyzing the details of his life and death. But there were some things she wished she could talk to someone about. Every day her guilt challenged her otherwise stable mind.

Agustina was glad to see Dr. Tonami when he drove up that afternoon. Even though his absence had been brief, he was her only daily connection to the real world, and she appreciated and respected his friendship. As usual when a guest was present, though, she did not say much but concentrated on her work.

"Agustina, this is Alejandro Sanchez." Dr. Tonami introduced the tall, handsome, middle-aged man, who extended his hand. In the Japanese style to which she had become accustomed, Agustina did not look up but bowed slightly, rubbing her hand against her apron before extending it to shake the hand that was waiting for her.

"'Welcome to Dr. Tonami's home, Mr. Sanchez," she said. She didn't want to show her excitement over having a guest, but couldn't keep from looking at him. She thought that his distinguished light wool suit was perfect on his tall frame, and his baritone voice was consistent with his dark good looks.

Dr. Tonami had invited other detectives home before but very few had Spanish surnames. The fact that Mr. Sanchez was obviously Hispanic made her feel more confident of the meal she had waiting for them. She excused herself and returned to the kitchen.

Agustina's mind was full of questions. The detective had made a strong impression on her. His hand was soft and gentle and his height impressed her. He reminded her of her father — same voice and presence. He even had a bushy mustache like her father's.

Agustina wondered if the detective had ever seen other young men like Diego die in their own spit. She pinched herself to keep her mind from wandering, and went back to the library to offer the men two tall glasses filled with ice and *orchata*, sweet rice water. This was Dr. Tonami's favorite drink during the summer. It was a Mexican drink that Agustina's mother taught her to make when she was in the eighth grade. By now, she had perfected her *orchata*-making skills, knowing the exact pinch of this and that to make it pleasing to everyone.

As she had imagined, the two men had removed their jackets and folded them across the backs of the library's brown leather chairs. They stood next to the small conference table, where Dr. Tonami had unrolled several large crime scene photos of the case they were working on. She knew they would study the photos meticulously in preparation for their court testimony. Agustina entered quietly and placed the glasses of *orchata* and the tray of fruit and vegetables on the broad wooden windowsill facing the garden.

"Is there anything else I can do, Dr. Tonami?" she asked, hoping to be included in more conversation with the detective. She felt slightly silly hoping for such an outcome.

"Thank you, Agustina, this is fine. We'll have dinner about six."

Agustina left the library as quietly as she had entered. She felt lonely for Dr. Tonami's company but had always respected his time with his guests. She knew that dinner was the only event that kept her under the same roof on this occasion, so she stayed quiet and out of the way in the kitchen.

Detective Sanchez had also hoped that Dr. Tonami might include Agustina in the conversation. His keen skills of observation had taken in the details of his host's housekeeper, and he could tell that she was intelligent and lonely.

Agustina felt important to be in Dr. Tonami's home and was glad to be of service to such a good man. She was so grateful that he traveled to Mexico when Diego died. His visit had been an unexpected surprise and one that sealed her admiration for him. The memory of Dr. Tonami in Mexico made her want to cry, but the time was not right for such emotions to be displayed. Instead she began to cut the lettuce for the tacos, along with fresh red tomatoes and onions. As she cooked the refried beans, she grilled a shank steak under the broiler.

Despite the menu, the meal would be served as usual at the low Japanese table. Dr. Tonami had already prepared his guest by asking him to remove his shoes at the doorway. Also as usual, Agustina set out both chopsticks and forks. The lettuce, chopped tomatoes, and onions were presented in a Japanese *bento* wooden dish along with shredded cheddar cheese. The beans were served in a ceramic Japanese bowl, and each man had an individual ceramic bowl of steaming white rice at his place. Agustina radiated with pride as she laid the beautiful, fragrant meal on the table.

Dr. Tonami wanted a beer with dinner and Mr. Sanchez thought that sounded good. Dr. Tonami liked to drink his beer from a heavy stein. The detective just wanted his beer in the can. The two men sat crossed-legged, enjoying their dinner as Agustina walked back and forth from the kitchen to make sure they had everything they needed.

After they took second helpings she served herself two tacos and some beans and sat at the small wooden table in the kitchen to eat. She was just biting into her second taco when she heard the men getting up from the floor. She had not yet served the hot tea and green tea ice cream that Dr. Tonami enjoyed at the end of a meal. She pushed her chair back and hurried after the men as they headed toward the library.

"Did you want anything else?" she asked.

"I'd have another beer, please." Detective Sanchez turned to look her straight in the eyes. Agustina ducked her head and turned to get another beer from the refrigerator. His eyes surprised her — so deep and dark, just like his mustache. She placed the cold beer on her round wooden serving tray along with an empty glass in case he wanted it, and held it up for him to take. This time she did not avert her gaze.

"*Gracías*, Agustina," the detective said in his deep, friendly voice. He sounded so much like the radio disc jockey on the morning show that played Mexican music.

"*De nada*," she responded, and shyly returned to the kitchen.

The dirty dishes were minimal now compared to when all the children were still at home. These days were like vacation days for Agustina. To serve and clean up after so many people had not been an easy task, but she found herself missing the days when the two families had been together at meals.

The sound of the telephone shook her from her mental digression. She could hear Dr. Tonami on the phone in the library. She assumed it was probably one of his sons calling from the university. They often called after dinner, and always asked to speak with her as well. Agustina dried her hands on a towel in anticipation of Dr. Tonami's signal for her to pick up the extension in the kitchen.

"Agustina, please come here," he called to her. Puzzled, she hurried to the library.

"Yes?" She thought Dr. Tonami looked nervous.

"I need to leave for UCLA. Tom was in an auto accident and he's been taken to the university hospital." Dr. Tonami was already packing his medical bag. "Mr. Sanchez can remain here to work on our case. Please make sure he's treated well." As he put on his jacket he apologized to the detective for leaving him, but nothing was more important to him than his sons. He still adored them as if they were little boys. "Call me at the hospital if you need anything."

"Please call us as soon as you can to let us know how he's doing," Agustina asked as Dr. Tonami rushed out the door. She could tell that the injuries must be serious for him to take his own medical bag along.

The detective had already turned back to the photos on the table. Agustina watched as he analyzed the gory pictures and made notes in a loose-leaf notebook. The horrific photos immediately reminded her of Diego.

"Can I get you something else, Mr. Sanchez?" Agustina asked before excusing herself.

"*No, gracías, estoy bien.*" He was obviously caught up in his work, but Agustina wanted to hear more of his voice.

"*¿Habla Español?*" she asked, caught off guard by his few clear words of Spanish.

"*Claro, soy Mexicano.*" He acknowledged his Mexican heritage, and turned to smile at Agustina. "*¿Y usted?*"

"*Yo, tambien soy Mexicana-Americana, de padres Mexicanos.* My parents came to California and worked for Dr. Tonami's family," she added in English, "and I was born on his father's ranch. Let me know if I can bring you anything," Agustina said as she left him to his work.

• • •

AGUSTINA FINISHED HER INDOOR CHORES more quickly because her mind was occupied with thoughts of the detective. She noticed the sun was beginning its unstoppable course toward sunset, and went out to feed the fish. The horizon was lined in bright oranges and yellows, but the pond still reflected the blue sky. The exotic fish seemed to peek out of the water for a glimpse of the setting sun as they reached for morsels of food.

Agustina tossed the pellets in the water at intervals, waiting to see how quickly the previous handful were devoured by the hungry fish before she gave them more. As she dug into the plastic pail of food in her lap she noticed that Mr. Sanchez was watching her through the window. He was smiling broadly as if he approved of the way she fed the colorful animals. As she tossed the next handful of food into the water, the detective came out through the kitchen door and into the garden. He stood next to Agustina and watched as she untangled pellets from the waterlily leaves.

"May I sit down?" he asked.

"Sure," she replied. He sat next to her and she quickly tossed another handful of pellets. "The pond and the sunset are very soothing." Agustina was nervous and lost track of the timing of her tosses. As much as she longed for conversations with other adults, the reality of this one had already unnerved her.

"Those fish are hungry things," Mr. Sanchez commented. "Dr. Tonami has a beautiful home and garden," he added, looking around at the well-kept grounds. "He praises you for your hard work, Agustina."

She was surprised by that remark but didn't want to act as if it were unexpected. "Thank you," she tried to say gra-

ciously, but her cheeks were blushing with the embarrassment of appreciation. She was surprised that Dr. Tonami
had mentioned her to the detective. "I should be the one
saying nice things about Dr. Tonami. He has been good to
me and my family," she said. Agustina could smell the
detective's perspiration and his cologne all at once. His
once-crisp white shirt had already gone through more
than a day's worth of work.

"Would you like me to wash and iron your clothes later?"
she asked. As soon as she spoke, it dawned her that he
had probably brought a suitcase or a garment bag.

"Oh no! You just reminded me that my bag is in Dr.
Tonami's trunk. But I'm sure that he'll get back before
morning," Mr. Sanchez said as he grabbed a handful of
the fish food to toss. "Thanks for asking, Agustina," he
added.

It was obvious to Agustina that the detective was a decent
individual. He was not pretentious at all. She wondered if
he had ever gone through a difficult personal situation,
something outside work. She really was curious about the
handsome voice that seemed so similar to the one on the
radio. She wanted to ask him a million unnecessary questions, her hunger for conversation was so great. She

wished she was still young enough to talk effortlessly. When she was young she had not been afraid of much. It was not until after she became pregnant with Diego that she realized life wasn't filled with joy and happiness. Now she thought young people had no way to measure happiness or danger or anger. The fear of reality and the holding back of emotions come with age, she decided.

Agustina felt unattractive, too. She had gained weight after childbirth and the years had added on to that. She had gone from a size eight to a size fourteen. Under her real chin was a fatty layer of skin that was beginning to hang loose. Most of her extra weight had accumulated on her hips. But the television news often reported that women with pear-shaped bodies were less likely to have heart attacks than women who were top-heavy, so she consoled herself with that. Agustina realized that her mind was wandering again, and gave herself a little pinch on the arm.

"Dr. Tonami said you lost your son not too long ago. I'm sorry," Mr. Sanchez said. Agustina was shocked to hear him speak of her son. A cold chill rushed from her head to her toes after he spoke of Diego.

"Diego was not a very good young man, but he was my

son," she said, trying to find out exactly what he knew. She knew that Diego would be watching, perhaps through the eyes of the fish or through the flowering magnolia tree that shaded one end of the garden. Agustina always felt that Diego was around her, watching her every step.

"Do you have any children, Mr. Sanchez?" She dared to ask a stranger such a personal question because he had piqued her curiosity, and she was ready to accept the type of response that told her not to ask.

"Please call me Alejandro," he replied, and then sighed deeply. "I don't have any children. I wanted to, but my wife told me that the doctors said I couldn't have children," he said frankly. "She passed away three years ago after a long fight with multiple sclerosis." Detective Sanchez volunteered more than she had expected.

"I'm so sorry about your wife," Agustina said. "It must be very painful to go through what you have endured," she added, hoping that he would ask again about her son. A look of lament in his eyes made Agustina feel close to him. *Maybe he understands what it feels like to go through what I went through in the last few years*, she thought.

"I got over it. Life gives and takes and you don't know

why it happens. I reached the point where I didn't ask," he said, shaking his head slowly. He stared at the darkening pond. "Sometimes, you pay the price of the past, and you don't know why you're facing the drama until you pull apart the many layers of curtains of the past." Mr. Sanchez spoke like a man with a heavy heart. He sounded very wise to Agustina.

"Would like you something to drink?" she asked in effort to lighten his mood.

"I'll go get myself a beer if you don't mind." When she didn't object he stood and walked to the house. Agustina figured he was upset now and wouldn't come back to the garden. She began to tie the ends of the plastic bag into a knot. The fish did not like soggy food. In many ways the fish had helped her get through her difficult life with Diego, and she wanted to be good to them in return.

When Agustina felt the detective's presence at her side she jumped up so that he could sit. "Oh, please don't stand," he told her. He held a beer in one hand and a goblet in the other. "I brought you a glass of the white wine from the refrigerator," he said politely. Agustina thought she should refuse the wine, but did not want to appear rude. She had not had wine to drink in ages — not since that memorable night when Diego was conceived. She also felt guilty that the maid of the house was talking with a guest.

"*¡Salud!*" Mr. Sanchez raised his beer, obviously expecting her to respond. Agustina hesitated, as she did not remember ever being treated like such an adult. She raised her glass and smiled as the tin can and the goblet touched.

"How about you? Do you have a husband?" he asked her. "Actually, you don't have to answer that question. I know the answer because Dr. Tonami told me you never married," he said as he raised the can of beer to his lips for another big gulp. Agustina watched his Adam's apple bob vertically with each swallow.

Well, at least he's honest, she thought. But she was a little suspicious. "What else do you know about me?" she asked.

"I promise, that's all I know. No more questions. I promise," he said reassuringly. Detective Sanchez realized that he had made Agustina uncomfortable. He was used to asking a lot of questions in his line of work, and found it difficult to relax.

Agustina believed him when he said that he knew nothing else. Without asking permission, he got up and went inside for another beer. She took a tiny sip of the wine and then tipped the glass so the bushes by the pond could have a big sip. She was not inclined to drink wine but was enjoying the company of the visitor.

Mr. Sanchez came out again with another can of the beer. They moved from their perch at the side of the pond to a wooden bench close by.

"What brought you here?" he asked her. Agustina wasn't sure he understood that she was the maid. But something was different about this guest, this time, and she felt the need to be social to compensate for Dr. Tonami's absence.

"Circumstances of life brought me here," she began, and immediately felt uncomfortable. "My father, he sent me to Dr. Tonami." That sounded bad, too, and she felt guilty for not wanting to blurt out the entire truth. "I'd better go get the rest of my chores done," she said with resignation, and raised herself from the bench.

"Oh, please, don't leave," the detective begged her. "Dr. Tonami will be back soon and he wouldn't appreciate it if you were a poor host to his guest." He was teasing her, but she knew he was right. She was uncomfortable with his questions, though, and wished that she knew how to avoid the sensitive issues. She really enjoyed his company and wanted to stay. He gently grabbed her arm and pulled her back down to the bench.

"Would you like another glass of wine?" he asked when she pretended to take another sip. "Here, let me freshen your glass." Before she could object, he was on his way back to the kitchen with her wine glass in hand. He returned quickly with it filled to the rim. As he neared the bench, the phone rang. Agustina jumped up and rushed past him, trying hard to stay on the narrow Japanese path. Their bodies brushed as they tried to squeeze between the decorative plants on either side of the flat rocks.

Dr. Tonami was calling from the hospital. "How's Tom doing?" Agustina asked with much concern. She was sad to hear that Dr. Tonami was staying at the hospital for the night. His son needed immediate surgery for a compound fracture of the leg, and Dr. Tonami was going in with the surgical team. He gave Agustina specific instructions to care for his guest and make sure that he had everything he needed. Agustina assured him not to worry about the detective. She would take care of everything. They bid farewell and she returned to the garden.

"How is Dr. Tonami's son?" detective Sanchez asked.

"He's having emergency surgery on his leg," she responded. "Dr. Tonami won't be coming back tonight because he's going to be part of the surgery team," she added.

"That's too bad," Mr. Sanchez said, shaking his head. "He's a good man and he doesn't need any more worries right now. Knowing how he worries, I'll bet he told you to make sure my stay here was comfortable," he added, laughing. Sheepishly, Agustina laughed too.

It felt awfully good to laugh out loud, she thought. It had been a long time. Agustina took a tiny sip of the cool wine and smiled at the guest for making her laugh. She knew he was too smart for her to say the wrong thing or to try to give him a misleading response. His job depended on how well he was able to read people and how well he listened to the inconsistencies anyone blurted out, including her own.

The mustachioed detective was very handsome, she thought suddenly. Agustina noticed the lines under his eyes that crinkled when he laughed. She wondered if his wife had ever followed the lines with her index finger as they cascaded to the sides of his smiling mouth. She took another sip of the wine and decided it tasted good. He emptied another can of beer. The guest was happy and so was she.

Agustina was feeling a little more at ease because the detective was so down to earth. A fleeting worry that she was keeping him from his work was replaced by the realization that he was assertive enough to be inside working if that's what he needed to do.

"How about your parents?" Agustina asked, wanting to even the information score.

Mr. Sanchez turned toward her and laid his long arm along the edge of the bench behind her back.

"My mother lives here in Pico Rivera," he said. "My father passed away many years ago, while I was in the Army." He took a long drink from his beer. "My mother is in her eighties but she is really a firecracker in spirit." He smiled to himself at the thought of his mother's energy. "You should go with me to visit her sometime," he suggested as though they'd been friends for ages. "She's a lot of fun." Agustina did not know what to make of the invitation.

"I can't do that." She responded without much thought. In

a way it sounded like fun, but she had never visited anyone in town before. Diego had taken up all her energy.

The sun had disappeared beyond the horizon and the automatic sprinklers began to pour their huge drops all around the couple.

"That means it's time to go inside," she told the detective. Agustina was just barely feeling the effects of the alcohol, but she knew it could get worse. She stood up and reached for the empty beer can, but he held on to it tightly and took her empty wineglass as well. He led the way along the path to the house, stopping before the entrance to hold the door for her.

"Ladies first," he said, smirking at the old-fashioned phrase. Agustina couldn't remember when anyone had ever held a door for her. It felt very special. She wondered if he had held doors for his wife. His attention made her feel like a queen.

She showed him where to throw away the empty cans and then offered to show him his room. The space looked clean and orderly, and Agustina was proud of her handiwork. Knowing that his bag was still in Dr. Tonami's car, she volunteered again to wash and iron his clothes. She also gathered some shaving tools for his use, and found one of the boys' old robes for him to wear. The detective towered over Dr. Tonami, so the younger man's robe was a better fit. Then Agustina politely excused herself.

From her guesthouse, she could see the lights on in the study. She guessed he was probably working on the criminal case. The wine made her feel lightheaded, so she laid back on her bed. She must have been asleep already when she heard a firm knock. Then she remembered the detective, and went to the front door and opened it a crack.

"Agustina, it's me, Alejandro, your guest," he said with a laugh. Agustina froze for a second, then opened the door. "You know, it's only eight o'clock," he said as he stepped inside. "May I come in?" he asked, after the fact.

"Sure, come in," Agustina couldn't believe what she was doing but she knew she was a little high on the wine. She felt different. Her body was very relaxed.

"I finished my work," he said as he looked around the kitchen. "I really came to bother you for a little more of your time," he said apologetically.

"What you're saying is that you're lonely." Agustina

placed her hands on her hips like she used to do with Diego when he was trying to trick her into believing something unusual.

"You know, Agustina, I thought about this. I'm a fifty-one-year-old man who doesn't have a wife or even a girlfriend. I am lonely, I admit it. I didn't expect to meet someone like you. You truly are a very nice woman," he stated convincingly. He had the most handsome smile and a clear twinkle in his eyes as he spoke to her.

"I really don't what to say, Alejandro." She was playing dumb, but she was lonely, too. Who was she kidding? Ever since Diego died, she couldn't go to sleep without feeling the need to be held. She wasn't young anymore, but her body was still responding to the detective's masculine overtures.

She had never had any experience with men other than her sad night in the desert during high school. Despite all the romance novels she had read, she could not imagine herself in such situations. Life had dealt her another set of cards. She could not see life dealing from a new deck now that she was almost forty-six.

Suddenly Alejandro took her in his arms and held her

tight. Agustina felt like lard melting away into liquid over a hot fire. She was nervous but liked the way she felt, and figured she had nothing to lose. They stood that way for several minutes, not saying anything as if they were transferring messages through the warmth of their bodies. The detective caressed her hair with his hands, and Agustina rubbed his back in response.

"I like you, Agustina," he said several times as he stroked her. She did not answer, but concentrated instead on the euphoria she was feeling.

Alejandro lifted her easily and carried her into her small bedroom. He tenderly put her down beside the bed and engulfed her in his arms again. Agustina felt herself let go, wanting to be fed like she fed the fishes — slowly, patiently, and with care. She was exhausted from a lifetime of self-imposed misery. It was her turn now to relax and blossom.

7

Chapter 7

In the morning she opened her eyes and felt the Virgin of Guadalupe looking at her knowingly. Agustina's bare body gave her an immediate reminder of the previous night's events. She propped herself up on one elbow and looked around the room. Her clothes were neatly arranged on the chair. Alejandro must have picked them up from the floor, she thought. Maybe the wine had deepened her sleep, as she could not recall how long he stayed in her room. How could she face him this morning? And what if Dr. Tonami had already returned? Agustina panicked. She should cook breakfast for his guest right away.

"My Lady," she prayed to the Virgin over and over again, shaking her head in remorse. "How could I let myself go for such bodily pleasure?" The tears flowed from her eyes. She remembered that the last time she indulged herself she was stripped from her family and sent away. She prayed for forgiveness.

She was embarrassed to have to face the detective again.
Why had he done it? Was he really lonely? She was con-
fused and feeling guilty when she stepped into the shower.
Tears and water rolled down her cheeks at the same time.
She looked angrily at the cellulite on her legs as if to say,
"What are you doing there?" She had not been so aware
of her physical self in a very long time.

Meekly, she walked to the main house to begin her chores.
As she passed the bench by the pond, she winced at the
memory of the wine. But as she entered the kitchen, her
smile returned in spite of her anguish. The table was set
for breakfast and the house was filled with the spicy aroma
of fried sausage. Alejandro had cooked a large omelet for
both of them. He smiled broadly as he welcomed her into
the kitchen. Two tall glasses of freshly squeezed orange
juice waited on the table, and the coffee was already
brewed. There was not one dirty dish in the sink.

"Please come and sit down," he said, pulling a chair out
for her. He had a large kitchen towel hanging from his
arm, butler-style, and Agustina could not contain her
laughter.

"I'm the one who should be cooking," she told him. "Dr.
Tonami wouldn't like this."

"But the doctor is not in, so please, have some toast." He politely took her hand and guided her to her seat. He handed her a plate with perfectly toasted bread buttered on both sides. *This man knows how to cook*, she thought.

"I want to apologize for what happened last night, Agustina," he said, and then shook his head. "Listen to me! I like you, and here I am apologizing for liking you. I think I must be getting old. What I want to say is that I'd like to take you out and get to know you better."

"Señor Sanchez, I'm the one who should apologize. I should never have had that glass of wine. I beg you not to mention a word of this to Dr. Tonami." Her pleading voice was convincing. She was afraid that if Dr. Tonami knew what had happened, he would never trust her again.

They were eating breakfast in silence when Dr. Tonami walked in the house looking worn out from his ordeal. Agustina and Detective Sanchez stood to greet him.

"How is your son?" Mr. Sanchez asked.

"I'm glad Agustina has taken care of you this morning." The doctor responded almost as if he had not heard the question. "My son's surgery went well. I must apologize for leaving an invited guest," he said as he dropped his medical bag by the door and sat down at the table.

"Can I fix you some breakfast, Dr. Tonami?" Agustina asked.

"Just some coffee, thank you," he responded. "Did Agustina treat you well, Alejandro?" Dr. Tonami looked at his guest and then at the remnants of the hearty breakfast. He assumed Agustina had cooked the meal.

"She is an exceptional cook and housekeeper," the detective answered, and then winked quickly at Agustina. "She washed my laundry so that I could have clean clothes this morning," he added.

Agustina wondered why he said that she washed his clothes when she had not. As she carried her dishes to the sink she peeked into the laundry room and noticed the soap was in a different spot. Detective Sanchez had washed his clothes himself.

"I apologize for not remembering that your overnight bag was in the trunk of my car," Dr. Tonami said. "Thank you, Agustina, for helping our guest feel at home." She refilled their coffee cups without saying a word.

After breakfast, Dr. Tonami took the detective back to the library. Agustina could tell that Dr. Tonami was very tired and had probably been up all night. When the two men returned to the library, she walked outside to visit the fish and clear her mind. It was the first morning in twenty-eight years that something other than Diego had been a priority in her mind. She tried to ignore the dampness between her legs, but felt guiltier than ever.

After a while she walked back to the house to begin her chores and plan a meal for lunch. The men emerged from the library and surprised her with their plans.

"Agustina, I'm going to take a brief rest before I head back to the hospital to see Tom," Dr. Tonami said as he picked up his coat and bag and turned toward the stairs. "Mr. Sanchez has informed me that you are invited to visit his mother in town. I think that's a very good idea since I will not be here for lunch," he said, and disappeared upstairs. Agustina's mouth hung open in amazement. It irritated her that this man she hardly knew was trying to control her life, making plans for her without asking.

Quietly, she followed the detective back to the library and watched him gathering the photos and other data to put them away. Her hands were on her hips and her lips were pursed. She was ready to explode with a torrent of anger about the day's plans and a few other things, too.

"Before you say anything," he began, placing his index finger over her lips while he whispered to her so that Dr. Tonami would not hear the commotion, "please don't be mad. Dr. Tonami told me you needed time to unwind. He said you'd had some stressful times lately. A visit to my mother's house will be very relaxing. I promise!"

Agustina was speechless. She knew that she couldn't work in the house while Dr. Tonami was trying to rest. Perhaps visiting this man's mother would distract her from her guilt. She prayed to herself as she walked to her house to get ready. Her prayers calmed her uncertainty.

"Can we leave in twenty minutes?" Alejandro asked apologetically. He could tell that she was troubled about going with him. She nodded her assent as she walked past him. Agustina thought the fish in the pond were staring at her as if they wanted to say something. Perhaps they thought she was about to do something she shouldn't, she worried. But Dr. Tonami had encouraged her to go. Maybe this was his way of telling her that she needed a break.

The first thing she did when she entered her house was to

go straight to the Virgin and pray for guidance and protection. She was filled with fear and guilt about how quickly Dr. Tonami's guest had become close to her. Her heart swelled with emotion when she let herself recall what had happened between them, but at the same time she felt as though she had been poisoned.

She took out the matches she kept behind the painted plaster statue and lit a new candle as an offering to her patron saint. The bright flame flickered against the red, white, and green satin curtain that decorated the wall behind the altar, and its light calmed her somewhere deep inside. She rose slowly from her knees and walked to her closet to choose something to wear.

Soon there was a knock on the door, and she could easily visualize the detective waiting for her right on the other side of the wooden door. She told herself that the visit to his mother would be good for her — a distraction from the pain in her soul.

"Agustina, I'm glad you're coming with me," Alejandro said through the door when she didn't open it. "I know that you'll enjoy our visit with my mother. Unless you really don't want to go. In that case, just say so and I'll visit her alone." He waited patiently for a reply.

Agustina tried to compose her face and her thoughts, and then without a word stepped outside. Dr. Tonami had offered the detective the use of his second vehicle, a tiny old Toyota sedan the Tonami boys had used during high school. The engine was running and the passenger door was open.

Alejandro helped Agustina gather the ends of her colorful skirt into the car before he closed the door for her. She sat rigidly in her seat with her legs pressed tightly together. She wished she had kept her legs together the night before, but it was too late. It occurred to her that Diego had many times ridden in the same seat she was now occupying, and a cold chill spread over her at the sudden memory of him.

When Alejandro stopped at the neighborhood store to buy his mother some groceries, Agustina went in with him and purchased a large bouquet of flowers. "She'll like those very much," he called to her when he saw her waiting to pay in the checkout line next to his. Agustina smiled in spite of herself, knowing well how flowers make people happy. She could feel Alejandro staring at her, and raised the bouquet to cover her face as though she were inhaling the fragrance.

• • •

THE DRIVE TO PICO RIVERA WAS NOT A LONG ONE, and
soon Agustina and Alejandro were parked in front of a
small concrete-block home surrounded by many green
plants and blooming flowers. Several iron bird cages hung
inside the front porch, and singing birds flapped their tiny
wings as the two approached. Beneath the cages the
wooden floor was stained with many droppings.

"Mamá? Mamá?" Alejandro called loudly as he swung
open the screen door to enter the small home.

A weak voice responded from the living room. *"Aquí estoy,
hijo."* (Over here, son.)

Stepping inside the house, Agustina was amazed to see a
tiny woman barely four feet tall. She had expected
Alejandro's mother to be tall like him. But age and arthritis had crippled the older woman's body; the curvature of
her back bent her body toward the floor. Agustina could
see that she had been a taller woman in her youth. Now
the wrinkled, leathery skin of her face and hands revealed
the hardships that had bent her like a twig.

When she extended her weathered arms to welcome her
son, she looked to Agustina like a guardian angel. Her
long, white hair was combed into a loose bun, but wisps
stood out in all directions like a halo around her head.
The small half-apron she wore around her waist fluttered
as she struggled to walk. The soft fabric of her black cotton shoes made a whispering sound on the carpet with
each difficult step.

As the old woman wrapped her fragile arms around her
son's waist, he bent low to accept her love and kiss her on
the head. He hugged her very lightly and patted her gently
on the back. Agustina saw that he was on the verge of
tears and working hard to keep his emotions under control. He straightened up and cleared his throat, then took
his mother's aging hands in his as if they were expensive
crystal. Agustina could see the veins showing through the
fading skin of the old woman's hands, and knew that
Alejandro must be able to feel them, too.

That sudden insight made Agustina realize that she was
seeing the kind of love that she had missed so much — the
love between mother and son — and the tears she had
held back all morning broke free. The big salty drops rolled
off her high cheekbones, and she turned away to dry them
with her handkerchief before anyone could notice.

The walls of the warm home were graced with photos of children and grandchildren at various ages, and Agustina was distracted from her tears. The colorful frames were attractive, and it was interesting to see how the detective's mother had organized them progressively, from each child's youngest years to the most recent.

Speaking loudly so his mother could hear, Alejandro introduced Agustina as a friend and told Agustina to call his mother Rosa. The elderly woman was hard of hearing but it was obvious from her happy smile that she had understood. Agustina hugged her just as Alejandro had and also shook her hand. With her other hand she presented the fresh-cut flowers, and could tell immediately that Rosa was thrilled to have them.

For a brief second, the old woman reminded Agustina of her own mother. Her generous smile and warm welcome lightened the load on Agustina's shoulders, and right away Agustina was glad she had decided to visit her. Rosa pointed toward the altar at the far end of the living room and asked her son to get a vase for the flowers. Agustina was comforted to see the large statue of the Virgin of Guadalupe. In the time it took Rosa to walk to the altar, Alejandro had filled a vase with water and brought it back so that she could place the flowers in front of the Virgin. Then, holding her son's hand to steady herself, she knelt down on a pillow on the floor. She made the sign of the cross and tenderly pulled her son down to kneel with her. The fragile woman praying with her strong son was as perfect a picture as any Agustina had seen on the walls, and she felt blessed to be in the room.

It helped Agustina to see that the detective really was a kind man who loved his mother. She made up her mind to set aside her worries about the night before, and enjoy instead the security she felt in Rosa's house. The sight of the old woman kneeling despite her pain humbled Agustina, and she became determined to embrace the visit as a godsend that released her from her own suffering.

After a brief prayer, Alejandro helped his mother up and to the dining room table where she could sit on a sturdy chair. Agustina sat across from her, and the two women chatted easily about the flowers and their altars and many other things. While she talked Agustina could hear Alejandro in the kitchen opening and closing the refrigerator and the cabinets, putting away the groceries. It was obvious that he had done this many times and knew where things went. She heard the oven open and close, and realized he was preparing food.

Agustina loved hearing the old woman's stories of happiness, sadness, and suffering. Very few rewards besides the grandchildren had come to her in her long lifetime. Rosa pointed to a photo on top of the television and was beginning another story when her son came out of the kitchen and interrupted.

"Oh, Mama, please don't tell that story. Please?" Alejandro knew it was going to be a story about himself and he was embarrassed, the first time Agustina had seen that trait in him. She was delighted for an opportunity to learn more about the man she felt so guilty for knowing, and encouraged Rosa to go on. Alejandro returned to the kitchen and took something out of the oven. The fresh aroma of blueberries filled the house, and Agustina realized that he had baked a pie.

"That is my son, Alejandro," Rosa said, pointing a wrinkled finger first at the picture frame on the television and then toward the kitchen. "He is a hero. He went to the war in Vietnam and he got hurt." As she spoke, she lifted her apron to wipe tears from her eyes. She described for Agustina the lives he had saved and the wounds he had suffered, and how he stayed long after his required tour of duty in order to help his friends. It was not until a near-fatal abdominal wound put him in the hospital for many weeks that he finally decided to come home.

"He came home as soon as the hospital released him," Rosa continued, "and then he married, and then his wife died." She covered her eyes with her apron.

No wonder he left the room, Agustina thought. *What a very sad story.*

She listened to Rosa with respect and admiration for the compassion she showed others. Agustina felt selfish by comparison, and wished she had had Rosa's attitude when Diego was alive. She hoped that sort of understanding might still come to her with age.

Alejandro changed the mood and the subject when he brought the warm pie to the table. As they ate Rosa told stories about her husband and recalled his passing many years before. Alejandro gave Agustina a brief, knowing look when his mother insisted that she was capable of living alone. Like many older Mexican women and men, she did not approve of retirement homes or assisted-living communities. Her independence was important, and so she moved around her house slowly but managed to cook for herself. Alejandro mentioned to Agustina that he had many times offered to get his mother some domestic help, but that she would not agree to it. Rosa dismissed him again with a wave of her scrawny arm, and the three chuckled together.

The warmth of their laughter made Agustina wish that she and Diego had not lived so far away from her own parents. Having a grandmother's love and guidance would have been good for her son, she thought. She wished she could bring Diego to meet Rosa, and then remembered she was inventing a solution for a problem that no longer existed. Diego was dead and nothing could bring him back.

That jolt of reality made Agustina long to be back at home by herself, doing her chores in Dr. Tonami's house or sitting by the pond to feed the fish. She knew that Dr. Tonami was at the hospital, so she would have plenty of time to herself to think about everything that had happened in the last twenty-four hours. Alejandro could see that Agustina's mood had changed and so began to do the dishes and talk to his mother about what she would like him to bring her on his next visit.

As Agustina and Alejandro bent over to hug Rosa farewell, the old woman made the sign of the cross on each of their foreheads. Agustina felt blessed and immediately promised Rosa that she would visit her again, on her own. Rosa's other children lived too far away to visit their mother often, and Agustina knew that she could help her around the house.

"I want you to know that I've never taken anyone to my mother's house except for my wife," Alejandro said as they drove away. "Thank you for coming with me to see her. She really liked you and enjoyed your company," he smiled and winked at Agustina as if seeking her approval. "Now can I convince you to go to dinner with me one of these days?" When Agustina said nothing, he responded to his own question. "Great, thanks." He was an expert at reading people's emotions even when they were quiet, and could tell that she was deep in thought.

He drove in silence toward the Greyhound bus depot in downtown Los Angeles. Agustina was too overwhelmed by her own thoughts to make small talk about his trip home to Ventura. When he pulled the car in under the bright blue-and-white neon sign of the terminal, Alejandro began to thank Agustina again. He pulled next to the curb and turned on the emergency lights in order to spend a minute or two more with her. He put his arm around the back of her headrest and touched her hair with his hand. "I hope I can see you again," he said in a tone that melted

Agustina's heart. But she smiled and said nothing.

Alejandro sighed and got out of the car, and Agustina
scooted over to the driver's seat. He pulled his small bag
through the back seat window, and then stuck his head in
Agustina's window and gave her a kiss on the lips. He
pulled back quickly and headed for the ticket counter,
waving to her one more time before disappearing inside.

Agustina was astounded by his touch of affection, and
drove through traffic for half a block before she remembered to turn off the emergency blinkers. She was indig-
nant that he stole a kiss from her, but the touch of his lips
on hers had ignited a flame of desire that filled her with
loneliness.

8

Chapter 8

One Saturday morning several weeks later Agustina decided to visit the old woman who had touched her heart. Dr. Tonami had just left for a week in Japan, so Agustina's responsibilities were lighter than usual.

In a small bag she gathered onions, oranges, and squash, then packed a plastic container with cooked white rice and added that to the bag. She filled an empty vase with gladiolas from the garden. On the way there she stopped at the grocery store to get a fresh chicken to fry. Agustina knew that Rosa would welcome the visit and the goodies.

The trip felt therapeutic somehow, and Agustina was glad to be able to show the old woman some love and attention. Besides, she knew that Rosa would tell her more stories that reminded her of her own parents and grandparents. As she parked in front of Rosa's house, the birds on the porch began singing their welcome. Agustina rapped sharply on the wooden frame of the screen door, remembering that Rosa did not hear well.

"*¿Quién es?*" (Who is it?) a tiny voice called out. Agustina could hear Rosa struggle to her feet.

"*Doña Rosa, soy yo, Agustina,*" she said, realizing that Rosa might not remember her. Agustina opened the door and held it with one foot while she moved the bags and the vase from the porch floor. The old woman was waiting with open arms and a wide smile. Agustina put her parcels down again and rushed to Rosa's welcoming hug.

"*¿Dónde está Alejandro?*" the old woman asked. She remembered that Agustina had visited her with her son, and Agustina realized that Rosa thought she was his girlfriend and would know where he was. Not knowing what to say, Agustina simply changed the subject, asking the old woman if she was hungry. When Rosa nodded eagerly, Agustina took the bags into the kitchen and showed Rosa what she had brought her. She placed the vase of flowers at the altar, and then looked more closely at the photos on the walls while Rosa talked about each one.

The old woman told stories about her life and Agustina listened attentively, hoping to hear more about Alejandro. Rosa's parents had escaped Mexico during the Pancho Villa revolution, and took their family to work in the cotton fields of California. Rosa married the first man she dated and had eight children in a dozen years. After an hour passed, Agustina took Rosa's hand and helped her to a chair in the kitchen so that she could continue telling her stories while Agustina cooked. Agustina really wanted to hear more about Alejandro but did not ask. She hadn't heard from him since the day they visited Rosa together, and she hoped his mother would have some news of him.

Agustina cut up the vegetables and put them to boil in a large pot. While the soup simmered, she cut up the chicken and readied a cast-iron pan for frying. Soon the house was filled with mouth-watering smells, and within an hour the two women sat down to enjoy the home-cooked lunch. Agustina was proud of herself and thought it was the most delightful lunch she had made in many years.

After they had eaten their fill, Agustina helped the old woman back to the living room, where they chatted some more. Rosa pointed to a stack of albums bursting with photos, and asked Agustina to bring them to the couch so that they could look together. Agustina reached first for a leather-covered one under the television, and Rosa nodded and smiled as if it were her favorite.

The women turned the yellowing pages together and studied the photos of Rosa's family. There were five sons and three daughters. One picture was taken at a birthday party. Rosa was much younger and looked happy and festive with all her children surrounding her. Toward the middle of the fat album was the same photo as the one in the frame on the television: Alejandro in his military garb, a handsome young man whose bushy mustache was still dark. Agustina saw an opportunity to engage Rosa in conversation about her son, and asked when the picture was taken.

"This was right before Alejandro went to the war," Rosa said. "He had many girlfriends," she added with pride. "They liked to call him Ollie."

Rosa turned the page and began to describe a family reunion they enjoyed just after Alejandro came home from the war. She didn't notice that Agustina had turned pale at the mention of a young man called Ollie. The name of Diego's father had caused Agustina's heart to plummet to her toes. Even after all these years, the memory of him made her cold with remorse.

She was half-listening to Rosa's stories when a loose picture slid out of the back of the album and the image of a nervous young girl in a red satin skirt became visible. Agustina caught herself before she gasped out loud, but her pulse raced and beads of perspiration broke out on her face. She reached across Rosa to pull the photo out the rest of the way, knowing that what she was about to see was a scene from her own past.

There was Rosa's son, Alejandro — Ollie — with his arm around a girl with peroxided hair and borrowed clothes. Agustina felt sick. She was in the home of a woman she hardly knew, looking at a high school photo of herself she'd never seen before.

Ollie was not killed in Vietnam, as she had presumed. Diego's father was alive! And he had taken advantage of her a second time.

Agustina excused herself and rushed to the bathroom. She flushed the toilet several times to keep Rosa from hearing her sobs. Tissue after tissue dissolved in seconds from the release of her emotions. Finally, feeling as though her heart was lodged at the bottom of her gut, Agustina decided she could contain herself once more, and returned to sit by Rosa on the couch.

"Who is in this picture?" she asked, picking up the photo from where she had dropped it on the coffee table.

Rosa shook her head. "That picture and some others came in the mail after Alejandro went to Vietnam. He doesn't remember them." Agustina felt as if she had been thrown into a sea of ice cubes. *How could he not remember the night their son was conceived? Because he doesn't know,* she told herself, *and I'll make sure he never does.* Her spirit tightened with stubborn resolve.

Agustina asked Rosa where the other photos were. The old woman pointed toward the kitchen and told her to look in one of the bottom drawers. Agustina was dizzy from shock and crouched carefully to keep from falling over. She opened several drawers before finding one stuffed with old photos. She sat on the floor and worked quickly to scan the drawer's dusty contents. At the bottom of the pile was a portrait-size version of the smaller photo in the album. Although it was the same pose, seeing herself again with Ollie nearly paralyzed her.

While Agustina stared at the photo, her mind raced with revelations. *Oh my God,* she thought. *Rosa is Diego's grandmother. But Alejandro said that he couldn't have children. How can that be?* She returned the pictures to the drawer, and pulled herself up to lean against the kitchen counter for a moment. She knew she would have to work hard to keep her anguish hidden from the old woman.

Hoping that her face would not betray her, Agustina returned once more to the couch. Rosa hoped that they could continue looking through the albums, and pulled on Agustina's skirt and patted the seat next to her.

"*Si le gusta el retrato, se lo regalo,*" she said, offering Agustina the photo on the table. But Agustina was clearly deep in thought, and Rosa closed the photo album. She knew that something had happened by the way Agustina was trying to smile. "What's wrong?" Rosa asked sadly.

Agustina could not stand to stay there any more. "May I keep this picture?" she asked. She was so full of emotion that she had not heard Rosa offer her the photo. Agustina held the picture against her chest as she asked, hoping that Rosa would not look at it again and recognize her.

"*Si, si,*" Rosa assured her, but before she could ask any questions, Agustina apologized for not feeling well and said she would have to leave. Rosa urged her to stay and take a nap, but Agustina felt it was impossible to remain any longer in the home of her son's grandmother.

The phone rang just as Agustina was about to leave, and she could tell from the way Rosa answered it that Alejandro was on the other end of the line. Agustina hurried to get out the door, certain that Rosa would tell her son that she had been there to visit and cook. She did not want Rosa to call her to the phone; she did not want to talk to the stranger who had stolen her emotions twice in one lifetime. Agustina was ashamed that she had fallen twice for the same man, and the only one in her life at that.

It was hard for Agustina to see the road through her tears. Her legs were weak and her heart was beating faster than ever. She knew she should pull over but was afraid that someone might stop to check on her, and she did not want to speak to anyone. So she drove with one hand and wiped her eyes with the other, wondering if it had all been a bad dream. The picture she had taken from Rosa lay on the front seat facing down.

At home, Agustina threw the picture on the kitchen table and fell to her knees before the statue of Our Lady of Guadalupe. *How could you do such a thing to me?* she asked her patron saint. *Did you know all along this would happen?* The Virgin just smiled her consoling smile and Agustina's tears continued to fall until she was too tired to cry any more, and went to bed.

The photo reminding Agustina of her desolate past reappeared to her in her sleep. Images of bad times with Diego resurfaced to haunt her dreams. She saw her son pointing his finger at her as if to blame her for his life. Agustina cried in her sleep so loudly that she woke herself up, gasping desperately for breath. She got up and drank some microwaved milk to calm her nerves, then lay in bed thinking and staring at the ceiling in the dark.

She woke again in the early hours of morning, and for a brief moment forgot that her past had been resurrected. Then she realized that her eyes were red and swollen and her stomach cold and sore. She wished that time could be reversed so she would never have memories of the past again. The truth she had discovered had shattered her peace.

At the same time, she was curious to learn more about the father and family of her son. *But what good would it do now?* she thought. Her son was gone forever. *If he were alive, perhaps his father could straighten him out. Maybe his grandmother would give him encouragement to be a better person.* Getting out of bed, she lit a candle before the Virgin of Guadalupe and begged the saint to calm her anxiety until she learned more. Surely there was a reason she had met her son's grandmother.

What would my father say if he knew this now? Agustina wondered. *What kind of welcome would he give Alejandro?* When her pregnancy had been revealed, Agustina's father and brothers cursed Alejandro, though they did not know his name and called him others instead. If they could have, they would have killed him, or so they said. *Would they still feel that way now?*

What would Alejandro think if he knew Diego was his son? And what if Rosa tells him I took the photo? Agustina had many questions and very few answers.

She walked to the table where she had left the picture face down the night before, and with a trembling hand turned it over to make certain that she was not dreaming. She wanted to be sure that the bleached blonde in the pink chiffon blouse was really her. She noted with pride that Diego had her beautiful smile, and it was obvious that he and Alejandro shared the same dark, shiny eyes. She left the photo face up so that she could look at it as she passed by during the day.

9

Chapter 9

As Agustina fed the fishes after dinner, the phone rang in her small house. She left the bag of pellets at the edge of the pond and rushed inside. She assumed it was Dr. Tonami calling from Japan. *Maybe he's coming home early*, she thought hopefully.

To her chagrin, the caller was Alejandro, apologetic for not calling earlier to thank her for visiting his mother. He also wanted to know if everything was all right. His mother had told him that Agustina was sick.

Agustina told him she was feeling better, and then silently thanked God that Rosa had not understood the reasons for her pain. That meant Rosa had not recognized Agustina in the high school picture and had not mentioned it to Alejandro.

Alejandro did know that Dr. Tonami was in Japan and asked Agustina if he could come to visit her. She immediately made an excuse about having to leave town for a few days. She knew her lie did not sound convincing but she did not want to have to look into his eyes. The thought of seeing him again made her heart sink in the salty sea of her emotions. She worked hard to keep control of herself so that he would not hear her sorrow.

Listening to his beautiful voice, she remembered now how magical his eyes had been that night so long ago and how charming they still were. She was mortified that she had allowed the same man to enter her soul twice. Yet she wanted so much to face him and tell him how angry she had been for so many years. She wanted to tell him that she was kicked out of her home because of the pregnancy. She wanted to tell him how much she would have loved to have a family, a husband. She wanted to tell Alejandro the ways Diego resembled him.

Her tears started flowing out of control. With the palm of her hand she covered the telephone receiver while she used her handkerchief. Alejandro did not know what to think when he heard her muffled sobs. She finally cleared her throat enough to say a quick farewell and ended the conversation without any explanation.

Agustina's loud cries were infused with all the emotions she had swallowed over the years. Crying on the inside had been a routine of self-protection from her own misery. She felt that her tears were wasted if they merely fell to the ground, but had somewhere to go when she cried on the inside. Now they spilled out over the dam of her defenses. She grabbed a terry-cloth towel from the bathroom to dry her eyes, then fell on her bed and covered her face with a pillow.

She was overwhelmed by the loneliness she felt when she thought of her son. Pregnancies are supposed to be beautiful and shared, but Agustina carried Diego with sorrow and isolation. She did not have a husband to rub her belly or put his ear close to hear the child. She did not receive flowers and gifts after the birth, the way most mothers do. And her son did not have a father. Diego was born lonely, and he died lonely. How could she ever forgive herself for what she had done?

Several weeks passed and Alejandro did not call. She missed hearing from him. She wanted to visit Rosa again but felt she was not emotionally capable of going yet. She knew the old woman needed her help, but Agustina felt old herself, weak and tired. She expended all her energy crying, and was run down because of it.

Menopause was often discussed on talk-radio shows she listened to, and she knew she was the right age for its symptoms to be developing. In a way, Agustina welcomed the change. Her periods would be over, and she believed that she would be a stronger, more confident and mature woman. Yet menopause also seemed to her like a path to old age, and she worried that she would not be able to work as a housekeeper forever. Already arthritis hurt her fingers. She knew that she moved more slowly than she used to, and even had started taking afternoon naps whenever she could.

When more weeks passed and her mood did not improve and her bones began to ache, Agustina decided to tell Dr. Tonami that she wasn't feeling well. She had read about menopause in some of the books in his library, and hoped he would give her some vitamins and iron to restore her energy. He listened to her symptoms and then asked her to visit one of his colleagues, a woman doctor who specialized in women's medicine.

Agustina made an appointment and looked forward to the day when she would begin to feel better. But when it was time to visit the doctor, she became nervous. Dr. Tonami had always taken care of any medical problems she had. The gynecologist gave Agustina an exam that she had not had since Diego was born, and then drew blood from her right arm. She knew from watching television that at her age she should have regular mammograms and Pap smears, but all of that frightened her and so she had never done it. Her only medical experiences had been trips to the hospital because of Diego's violence.

Agustina explained to the woman doctor that she was going through menopause, that she felt sick and was tired all the time.

"Do you think you could be pregnant?" the doctor asked. Agustina laughed at such a ridiculous question.

"I'm forty-six years old! I'm in no condition to be pregnant," she said. The doctor looked at Agustina sympathetically and asked her to go in the restroom and provide a urine sample.

Inside the clinic's bathroom Agustina laughed at the possibility of pregnancy as she tore open the sterile towel. She wiped herself as instructed before urinating in the tiny plastic cup. *I'm too old*, she told herself resolutely.

She carefully placed the brimming cup on the sink while she finished urinating, and then washed her hands. Then she returned to the examination room to wait. Within a few minutes the doctor came in and closed the door.

"Agustina, the urine test indicates that you are indeed pregnant," she said. "About ten weeks along. I can show you with ultrasound."

"I can't be pregnant," Agustina said in disbelief. "I don't have a husband." She was sure the doctor had made a mistake. "How could a woman my age be pregnant?" The doctor's easy explanation was not comforting. Agustina knew from TV and magazines about women over 40 having babies, but she did not meet the profile. She was not youthful and glamorous.

"Have you been sexually active in the last few months?" the doctor asked, waiting for Agustina's affirmative answer. Agustina was too embarrassed to reply, and she felt faint.

"Oh no, please, no!" She began to cry like a small child, howling and choking through her sobs. She had been through so much that the sharp blade of this news cut straight to her heart. Instinctively she wrapped her arms around her abdomen.

The doctor helped Agustina to another exam room where they could confirm the pregnancy with a machine that showed something like moving X-rays of Agustina's belly. Lying on her back with her head turned toward the machine's monitor, Agustina could see a tiny spot in the middle of a small sack. "There's your baby," the doctor said.

The young couples in the waiting room were clasping hands in anticipation of this kind of news, Agustina thought. But who could she tell? Who could she turn to? She was so alone. If she really was pregnant, she wanted someone to hold her hand and wait on her. She was afraid to be alone again.

The doctor left the exam room so that Agustina could get dressed again. As she waited for the doctor to return, she realized that her second brief encounter with Alejandro had created another new life. She had just used the last tissue in the box to dry her tears when the doctor returned with a bag full of vitamins and pamphlets and other prenatal items for her.

"Are you going to be all right?" the doctor asked, patting Agustina on the shoulder.

"I'll be OK," she responded, hoping to get out the door before she started crying again. The doctor reviewed with her the rules about diet and nutrition and reminded her not to do any heavy lifting, then told her she would see her again soon.

At the front desk Agustina made an appointment to be checked in four weeks, and filled out the usual forms with medical history and emergency telephone numbers. She gave Dr. Tonami's name and number in case of an emergency. Her sisters and brothers lived too far away to help, and besides, she would be too embarrassed to tell them she was pregnant anyway.

Agustina cried all the way home thinking about how she would break the news to Dr. Tonami. Emotionally and physically exhausted, she walked into her small home and knelt before the Virgin. On a normal day her prayers would have flowed freely, but today she could not find the words to express her feelings. Her throat was so dry and her eyes so swollen that she was reminded of the times Diego had beaten her, and those thoughts made her so weary that she decided to lie down for awhile.

• • •

AGUSTINA WOKE UP WONDERING how a woman her age could spend an hour with a stranger and become pregnant. *But then, that's how it had happened to me the first time*, she reminded herself. She checked her abdomen to see if there were any changes, but what was going on inside was still hidden away. The only difference Agustina could think of was the wrinkled skin on her hands and face that she had not had the first time. Surely she was too old for this.

All day she sat quietly in her house and thought about what she should do. Early in the afternoon, the ring of the telephone jarred her thoughts. It was Alejandro, and he wanted to visit her. He knew she was alone because he had spoken to Dr. Tonami the night before. Without saying a word, Agustina started to sob. Alejandro was still talking when she hung up the phone. Within moments it rang again and again. Agustina pulled the cord from the wall, and the house was quiet once more.

Because Dr. Tonami was out of town until late, Agustina

stayed inside her own house and did her laundry. When she heard a knock on her door in the early evening, she put down the folded clothes she was carrying and hurried to let Dr. Tonami in. But Alejandro was on the other side of the door. The handsome man with the graying mustache carried a large array of colorful cut flowers wrapped in green tissue paper. He was confused by the look on Agustina's face.

"Agustina, how are you?" he asked as he offered her the flowers. When she stepped aside and turned away, he placed the flowers on the kitchen table, then gently turned her around to face him. Her eyes were filled with emotions he could not read.

"What's wrong, Agustina?" He was worried now. She could not reply through her tears. She wanted to say that there was nothing really wrong, just that he had turned her life upside down, but all that came from her mouth were sobs of sorrow. Alejandro held her close while she cried, and when she began to relax he helped her to the sofa. She could not stop whimpering.

"What is it?" he asked over and over. "Please tell me."

Finally, she began to speak softly. She began by telling

him that she had not been feeling well and thought she was going through the change of life. He nodded his head as if he understood that troublesome process.

"But I'm not going through menopause," she said in a stronger voice. She looked him straight in the eyes. "I'm pregnant."

"What's wrong with that?" he asked. "The child's father will be very proud," he added, trying to be gracious. Agustina was elated to have said the words out loud, but Alejandro seemed stupid and that made her angry. Didn't he realize the truth?

Well, she thought disconsolately, *I raised one child alone. I guess I can do it again.* She began to cry.

Alejandro looked at her in confusion, and not knowing what else to do, pulled her up from the couch and into his arms. His detective skills were failing him so far. For a moment Agustina lost herself as he held her close to his heart. Leaning comfortably against his wide shoulders made Agustina feel very good.

Purposefully, Alejandro stepped back and took a long look in Agustina's teary eyes, hoping to see an answer. His strong hands held on to her, and a cold chill passed between them. Alejandro's eyes glistened as reality began to dawn on him. At that point, Agustina knew she would not have to say much.

"Agustina, do you have a man in your life?" he asked, knowing the answer to his question. Agustina felt interrogated. She knew how detectives worked, since she had so many times answered their questions by lying for her son. But this time Agustina did not have to lie. She had no reason to protect or defend anyone. The thought of being honest brought a peaceful feeling deep in the marrow of her bones.

"The child in my body could only be yours," she said, sobbing between words. She wanted to tell him not to worry about helping, that she had had some practice raising his first son by herself. But she knew that would not come out right.

"It can't be my son," he said with distress. "I can't have children. It can't be." Alejandro pulled out his handkerchief to wipe the sweat from his brow.

Agustina waited silently and merely looked at him until he understood that she was holding him responsible for

fathering a child. Then, as though his knees had become
weak, he sat down at the kitchen table and asked
Agustina to do the same. Shadows of fear and confusion
passed across his face. He had always wanted to have
children but had not been able to. Now that his wife was
deceased, fatherhood was the last thought on his mind.
Quietly he leaned his head against the wooden table as
he collected his thoughts. Agustina could see that his
arms were covered with goose bumps.

She wondered what he would do or say next. She was not
going to ask him to take responsibility. She was a middle-
aged woman and could handle things herself. The purpose of telling him was simply to get it off her shoulders.
She did not expect him to interrupt his own life because
of her pregnancy. She was the one who would cope with
the midnight feedings, the doctor's visits, and all the other
details of raising a child — for the second time, at midlife.
Agustina was beginning to believe that she was the
unluckiest of all women on earth.

"I'm fifty-one years old," Alejandro said as he raised his
head from the table. "I'm too old to be a father." He stared
at her helplessly. Agustina had hoped he might be proud
and happy and concerned about her. Instead she got a
selfish response that drew a cold line between them. His

denial was even more painful than her father's disappointment so many years before. Agustina felt truly rejected.

"What are you going to do about it?" he asked as if he
was expecting her to get rid of the problem overnight.
Agustina could tell that the concept of "baby" had not yet
sunk in. He still believed that he could not father any
children. She wished Rosa could hear him.

"Are you sure I'm the father?" he asked with his eyes and
eyebrows and not his heart. Agustina stood up from the
table, walked to the front door and opened it. Staring at
Alejandro through swollen red eyes, she motioned for him
to depart.

"Mr. Sanchez, please leave my house," Agustina ordered
assertively. She was so hurt by his attitude and response
that she did not want to talk to him any more. With all the
dignity he could muster, Alejandro stood up and walked
out. Agustina was angrier still that he had nothing to say as
he left, and so she slammed the door almost on his heels.
Agustina had never slammed a door on anyone, and could
not remember when she had ever let her emotions come
through her so physically. She had always withdrawn when
Diego was violent. *But this man is a jerk*, she told herself. *I
have no reason to protect him from my anger.*

She threw herself on the bed for a good cry but quickly remembered that being so upset would not be good for the little thing inside of her. She went back to the kitchen and made herself some yerbabuena tea, the mint tea her mother always drank whenever she needed to be calmed. Soon she felt confident of her maternal capabilities and hoped she would never see or hear from Alejandro again.

For the next month, she continued to work as usual. In her third month of pregnancy, her waistline began to disappear. The elastic in her underpants cut deep red creases into her skin. Her afternoon naps became more frequent. Agustina knew she would have to tell Dr. Tonami soon.

One hot summer morning when she felt especially tired, Agustina decided the time had come. Dr. Tonami was working at home since he had been in court late the night before. She served his breakfast and then poured herself a cup of tea and sat down across from him at the low table.

Dr. Tonami looked at her across the top of his glasses and then put his chopsticks down. He reached for her hand and held it in his.

"You don't have to say anything, Agustina," he told her. "The doctor called me a few weeks ago to ask who should

be billed for your care," he said. "You know that I will
help you any way I can. You have been good to me and
my family and so were your parents to mine." Agustina
blushed at his words. The monetary cost of her pregnancy
had not even crossed her mind.

But she was glad for his support and even more grateful
that he did not ask her any questions. She knew that Dr.
Tonami had probably already guessed who the father
might be. Tears slipped from the corners of her eyes as
she thanked him for his help. Dr. Tonami could not handle emotions well, and did not lift his eyes to make contact with hers. As she left the table to carry the dishes to
the sink, she turned to Dr. Tonami to thank him again.

"I'm sorry you've been burdened with so many of my
problems," she said sincerely. Dr. Tonami nodded in her
direction and made a small wave of his hand as if it were
nothing.

10

Chapter 10

For the next five months, Agustina grew and grew. She kept all her medical appointments and made it a point to walk around the garden at least once each day to keep her energy up for labor.

She had stocked her home with all the things she would need for the first three months after the baby was born. She had also framed a small picture of Diego and hung it on the wall next to a photo of her parents. In a moment of confidence she had told her family of her pregnancy and was relieved that they were very happy for her. In an effort to redeem himself, her father had already sent several toys for the coming child. Now her only real disappointment was with Alejandro, the father of both of her children.

With six weeks to go, her stomach seemed to reach out farther than her footsteps. She was overwhelmed by the difference in her ability to handle pregnancy in middle age. Her pace was so slow that she felt sure the garden caterpillars were reaching their destinations more quickly.

She was just glad for Dr. Tonami's patience with her as she moved in slow motion through her chores. Dr. Tonami was distracted too: He had met a Japanese woman and was busy trying to impress her. Agustina was glad his life was more normal now. He was visibly happier.

It was late afternoon on a windy autumn day when Agustina was surprised by a knock on her door. It took her a minute to rise from the chair where she was perched, careful not to sit all the way back lest she never get up. Slowly she made her way to the door and opened it to find Alejandro holding a bouquet of white roses.

"May I come in?" he asked politely. Agustina did not know what to say. She just stood there, while her stomach seemed to reach out for the roses. Alejandro looked at her lovingly and waited for her to speak. But Agustina was distracted by the baby; its tiny feet and arms had begun to move as soon as Alejandro had spoken. Finally she motioned for him to come in.

"How is your mother?" she asked as she headed back to her chair. She had to sit down before gravity pulled her toward the floor. Her face flushed with embarrassment when she realized how she must look to Alejandro. She could no longer see her shoes.

"She has asked for you," Alejandro replied, still standing. "She said to tell you that she misses you." *And where have you been all this time*, Agustina wondered. Anger started to rise in her but she did not have the energy to use it.

"May I sit down?" he asked, almost as if he was ashamed to be there. Agustina looked at her belly with love and adoration. Her right hand never left her abdomen. She welcomed the baby she was carrying, and she knew now that the Virgin of Guadalupe had done something pretty daring.

Agustina wanted Alejandro to sit down but was too short of breath to move or even speak. He laid the flowers in front of the Virgin and made the sign of the cross. Something was bothering him and Agustina could see it. He could not hide his discomfort.

Slowly, he sat down on the floor right in front of her knees. She dreaded whatever it was he was about to say

as she was tired and did not have much patience for anyone. She began to squirm back and forth on the edge of
the chair, rocking the baby inside. Alejandro kept his head
down for awhile and then got up on his knees and
caressed Agustina's enormous belly.

"Do you remember that night that Dr. Tonami's son broke
his leg?" he began as he rubbed her gently. Agustina felt
so tired and Alejandro's hands were so relaxing that she
closed her eyes while he spoke. She did not want to say
much, but she knew exactly what he was talking about.

"Ever since you told me you were pregnant and that it
was my child, I haven't been able to stop thinking about
it," he said with sincerity and remorse. "I can't sleep at
night." *Does this man know what he's saying?* Agustina
thought to herself. *Does he know what it's like to try to
sleep in this condition?* She was the burdened one, but she
kept her exasperation to herself.

"I told you that I couldn't have any children," he said as
his eyes welled up. He took a deep breath as though it
was his last before the lid of a coffin fell over him.
Agustina opened her eyes, expecting the worst sort of
excuses.

"My life had been a major disappointment to me and my family." He lifted his eyes to meet hers. "I was the only man in my family who could not have children. I've spent my life blaming myself for the pain I caused my wife and my family."

The baby let Agustina know that she needed to change positions, and she shifted in her seat as quietly as possible. It sounded as though Alejandro really had something to say, and she did not want to interrupt him.

Alejandro sensed her discomfort and got up from the floor to help her from the chair and over to the sofa. Agustina was grateful. It was the first time that someone other than Dr. Tonami had offered to help her recently. But it would soon be over, she thought, and she would feel all right again.

Alejandro helped her onto the couch, where she rested her back against one of the arms. Then he pulled a chair next to her. Agustina wondered where the conversation was heading.

"I called my wife's doctor last month. I wanted to find out the truth," he said as if he was unburdening himself of

some guilt. He reached into his back pocket for his handkerchief, then rubbed his eyes and blew his nose.
Agustina did not know what to think. She was so lonely
and now this man wanted her compassion when she did
not have an ounce to give away.

"Agustina, I think I am the baby's father!" Alejandro suddenly burst out. Before he could explain himself he began
to cry like a small child. He fell low on his knees in front
of her again and wept like Diego had as a child. Tears
streamed down Agustina's face as she held him by the
shoulders. *This part was easy*, she thought. She knew she
could devastate him with the rest of her secret.

Agustina tried to get off the couch so she could put her
arms around Alejandro. She felt sorry for him and hated
to see a man his age weep so openly. Finally she placed
her hands on his head and begged him not to cry. He
reminded her too much of Diego.

Diego's young face smiled down at her from the photo on
the wall. It seemed to Agustina that her son had somehow
planned this reunion of parents. She knew, too, that
Alejandro felt the spirit of this new baby in his veins.

On her hands and knees, Agustina broke away from his embrace and crawled to the Virgin of Guadalupe. Alejandro followed her to the altar and knelt beside her as they prayed and wept together.

Agustina looked up at her olive-skinned Virgin and directed her silent prayers to her. She asked her to give Alejandro the strength he needed to face his past, and she asked her not to leave her alone for the rest of her life. She wept to think of dying alone without the help and support of family.

At last, Alejandro stood up and extended his arms to help her. Agustina felt a surge of relief to have the support she had never had before.

"Thank you," she said as she pushed herself up with his help. He pulled her toward him and held her as close as her swollen body allowed. Agustina hoped that Diego could feel the embrace of his father through her. When Alejandro started sobbing again her tears returned, and she felt weak from sadness and desire for love. And then she fainted.

• • •

WHEN SHE AWOKE she was lying on her back in bed and Alejandro sat like a guard dog by her side. He had been wiping Agustina's forehead with cool water hoping that she would wake up. She tried to speak but he placed his finger against her lips to quiet her. Just then there was a knock on the door, and Agustina hoped it was Dr. Tonami.

"Agustina, this is my friend Dr. Flores," Alejandro said as he brought a man with a medical bag into her room. "He's going to examine you." Alejandro stood at the far side of the bed so the doctor could reach Agustina. He took her blood pressure and other vital signs and looked her over from head to toe to make sure she was all right.

The baby jumped as the doctor placed his cold instruments on Agustina's belly. A little foot kicked out in reply.

"Look, Alejandro, your child is kicking in retaliation for my visit," the doctor laughed. Alejandro beamed with joy. The doctor took Alejandro's hand and placed it on Agustina's abdomen where the baby moved like a young whale in the birthing waters of Baja. Alejandro followed the little foot as it stretched from one side of Agustina to the other just below her protruding belly button.

"I think it's a boy," Alejandro announced through his tears. Agustina was amazed that the two men could act as if they both had known her for a long time. Perhaps it was Alejandro's profession that made him so open, she thought. He did not seem to be embarrassed. He looked at Agustina with love and compassion, and she glanced toward the Virgin to see if her patron saint was taking the scene in. As usual, the statue's eyes were filled with understanding and patience. *If only I could learn from her and be graceful in handling life!* Agustina wished.

"Agustina, you must not get out of bed until the baby is born," the doctor told her as put his stethoscope back in his bag. "You're very weak and need a lot of rest," he added, looking at Alejandro as if holding him responsible. *Little does this doctor know,* she thought. *Alejandro will be gone in a few minutes, and I will be outside feeding the fish.*

Alejandro walked his friend out to his car and Agustina was disappointed that she could not hear their conversation. The doctor was giving Alejandro instructions as though he were in charge of her medical condition and needs. When Alejandro returned to her room, she hoped it was to say goodbye and leave her alone.

"Would you like something to eat?" he asked her. Before

giving her time to respond he spoke again. "I'm going to make some soup and bring it to you here. You heard what the doctor ordered. You have to stay in bed."

Agustina was furious but knew she could not get up. She had already tried to move her legs and found that she felt too weak, almost paralyzed. It was probably her age, she thought. If only she were a little younger, she would not have to be in this situation. Despite the clatter of pots and pans in the kitchen, Agustina must have fallen asleep again, because Alejandro surprised her when he carried in a tray with a bowl of steaming soup and crackers. He helped her sit up so that she could slurp the vegetable soup and savor the large pieces of potato. She drank several glasses of water because her throat was hot and dry.

After he washed the dishes, Alejandro came back and sat in a chair next to the bed. He took Agustina's hand and held it in his, and when he spoke he sounded more in control of his emotions.

"Dr. Flores is a friend of mine," he said with a warm smile. "He spoke to the doctor who took care of my wife. It seems that I am capable of having children after all." He paused, hoping for a reaction from Agustina. "I can have children, Agustina," he repeated.

I know that, Agustina thought to herself. *I've known it for twenty-eight years.*

"I told you once that I couldn't have kids, but that was not the case," he continued. "You convinced me to check into it. It wasn't me who couldn't have children," he said sadly. "My wife was buried with a secret. She was the one who couldn't have children, and she was afraid to tell me for fear I would leave her.

"I called Dr. Flores and asked him to test my sperm," Alejandro added. His detective skills had paid off by relieving him from the overwhelming guilt he carried. "Agustina, this is my baby," he said as he smiled at her belly. "I don't know you well, but I want my child to have a mother and a father," he said. "I want you to move in with me so that I can take care of you. I want my family to get to know you and our child."

"I can't do that," Agustina replied immediately. "This is my home. My father kicked me out when I was seventeen and I've been here ever since," she explained, trying not to cry. She thought she could talk about the past without becoming upset, but she could still hear the judgment in her father's voice as if it were yesterday. "I won't leave. I can't leave. My son was raised in this house and I cannot

leave his memory behind," she added as she pointed to
the portrait of their son.

Besides, Agustina thought to herself, *I'm not in love with
you. I don't even know you.* Their two brief encounters
were painfully memorable to her, even though she had
made every effort to erase Alejandro from her mind.

Agustina could sense that he was lonely, and figured he
just wanted someone to take care of him, to cook meals
and wash his clothes. She was grateful for his help but
she really wanted to be left alone. When she didn't feel so
sick and weak perhaps she could sort it all out. Alejandro
let the subject drop and Agustina fell back into a deep
sleep.

11

Chapter 11

Alejandro took vacation days from his job to stay with Agustina until the baby came. He cooked and cleaned and stayed nearby in case she needed anything. She could not understand why he was taking care of her but had to admit to herself that she greatly appreciated his help. Sometimes they watched television and talked about what they saw on the news, and in the evenings he read to her until she dozed off. She realized after a week had passed and she still could not get out of bed without his assistance that she would not have been able to manage without him.

Alejandro was determined to be a father to the baby she was carrying. Agustina could feel the warmth of his love radiating toward her. Gradually, his constant attention became a welcome gesture. Each day after lunch she reached for his hands and encouraged him to rub her abdomen in a slow, circular motion. She closed her eyes

to enjoy the massage, and her affection for Alejandro
grew.

One night in late November Agustina felt the baby kick
hard, as if he or she were ready to get out into the real
world. Alejandro was thrilled to see little bulges of feet
and elbows stretching Agustina's belly. He warmed some
lotion in his hands and followed the movements, caress-
ing her skin ever so gently. Agustina's tears flowed as her
lonely heart reached out in search of his touch.

Alejandro knelt astride her on the bed and put his head
against her abdomen so he could hear and feel the motion
inside. His closed his eyes as he listened to the baby, and
the profound peace that passed over Agustina made her
wish that he would never get up or open his eyes. She
wanted Alejandro there forever. She could not say it,
though; it was too painful to speak of what she wanted
and needed.

Alejandro helped her to the kitchen for dinner and after-
wards helped her prop her legs up on the couch. She
could tell the delivery of her second child was close at
hand. Silently, she prayed to the Virgin to let the baby
come soon.

Outside, a strong thunderstorm drenched the city. The loud claps shook the house and rattled the windows. Alejandro helped Agustina to her bed and then, as usual, took a pillow and a blanket to the living room couch. He reminded her so much of Diego. His walk was sluggish, but when he stood still, his posture was assertive. As the rain pitter-pattered on the roof, Agustina recalled other stormy nights when Diego had called out to her. Though he grew to be noisy and troublesome, as a young boy he was afraid of thunder.

From where she lay on her bed Agustina could see raindrops run down the windowpanes. The thin streams of water reminded her of her own tears when her father sent her away to live with the Tonamis. Memories of Diego gathered in knots at the base of her throat, and she could not keep from whimpering in sorrow.

Suddenly she felt a jolt to her upper body right between her breasts, as though the child inside had stretched out to touch both ends of her body. Agustina lay as flat on her back as she could to give the baby room to move, but the pain caused her to cry out. Alejandro was at her side immediately.

"Are you all right?" he asked. She could barely see him in the dark, but the shadow he cast was just like Diego's. He sat on the edge of the bed next to her and carefully put his arms around her belly. For a moment, she thought that Alejandro really cared for her. But that couldn't be. She was just a woman carrying his child — his second child, to be exact, and he didn't even know it. There was no reason for him to know, she thought. The warm feeling of love and tenderness vanished like a flash of lightning. Agustina was truly confused by Alejandro's presence.

"The baby is kicking deep inside me," Agustina told him. A wail of pain escaped her again. "It's stretching out too far," she whispered. Alejandro took the baby oil from her night table and squeezed the liquid into his hands. He rubbed her abdomen gently and the baby grew quiet again. Agustina sighed with relief. She had forgotten about the discomfort the last weeks of pregnancy caused. Alejandro helped her to sit up, and pushed several pillows behind her back to give her support. Sitting up, she could see his strong silhouette, and realized that he was not wearing any pants.

"Instead of sitting up, would you rather have your back rubbed?" he asked. Agustina carefully rolled over to turn her back toward him. She knew that the pain would return, but in the meantime, she closed her eyes and welcomed his hands as they caressed her back. Slowly, she reached behind her to grab his arm and pulled it forward to wrap it around her, leaving him no option but to lie in bed with her. Alejandro carefully stretched his body against hers. For the first time in Agustina's life, she welcomed the feeling of a strong, warm body lying next to her. Her buttocks rested against his pelvis in a perfect fit.

Alejandro kissed her passionately on the neck and back. Agustina could feel a rush of emotion from him. His soul was about to engulf hers again, but this time Agustina longed for the hope of love to take her spirit and hide it deep in his heart. He helped her remove her nightgown and took off his shirt, then stretched out behind her again. Never before had Agustina felt so loving and open. Their lovemaking was careful, yet fulfilling. They slept soundly the rest of the night, and so did the baby.

They lay quietly together in her bed the next morning, waiting for the sun to shine. The early birds were singing their happiest songs. But Agustina's lower back was very sore. Inside her she could feel the tug of labor pains beginning. Alejandro rubbed her belly, and the birth of her new passion overwhelmed the sharp reminder of the baby wanting out.

Agustina felt loved and cared for by Alejandro. Could it be real? Was she dreaming? She hoped that her old reality would not jump in to interrupt.

Alejandro welcomed her to the morning with a long look deep into her tired eyes. "That was the best night's sleep of my entire life," he said with a smile.

When Agustina got up to use the bathroom, she noticed that the baby had dropped low in her womb. Soon she would give birth, and her life would change again. Alejandro offered to make breakfast but she didn't feel like eating. She sat on the edge of her chair with her legs apart, drinking orange juice and gazing at Diego's photo.

"You must miss your son very much," Alejandro said when he saw Agustina staring at the youthful picture of her son. Agustina bit her tongue to keep the words from leaving her mouth. "What did you say his name was?"

"His name was Diego." She stood to touch the picture, to let Diego know that she had not forgotten him. She ran the tips of her fingers down his shiny cheeks. "I miss him very much, but he is doing better now," she added. Tears welled in her eyes. In some ways, she missed him so much.

"I feel for you Agustina, and I know what you mean," he said as if he had helped her raise him. "I run into troubled young men like Diego almost every day."

"What do you mean?" Agustina asked him. She wanted to know what he knew about her son.

"When your son died, Dr. Tonami was in the middle of helping me with a really difficult case," he said. He took a drink of coffee and the black liquid dripped from the mustache hairs above his lip. His words caught her by surprise.

"I didn't know it was your son who had died in Mexico until I came here months later to work on another case with Dr. Tonami and he told me you were Diego's mother. That was when I first met you," he said matter-of-factly. "I remembered the day that Dr. Tonami went to Mexico because he had been scheduled to give testimony in one of my cases and we had to ask for a continuance until he was back in California," he added.

Agustina recalled none of what he was telling her, only that she had been surprised by Dr. Tonami's sudden appearance at her parents' home in La Flor.

"Dr. Tonami has been my best friend for many years," Agustina said. "He is a kind man, and a very smart one."

"He is," Alejandro agreed. "I wasn't surprised to see the evidence he gathered," he added nonchalantly, assuming she knew what he was talking about.

"What evidence? What are you talking about?" Her eyes flashed with fear.

"Well, I mean regarding the circumstances of his death," Alejandro said and patted her on the arm. Quickly, he stood up to rinse his cup in the sink. Agustina was not ready to let go of the discussion. She was afraid to hear it, but she wanted to know everything he knew. She realized that Alejandro was behaving the way Diego had when he had information she wanted. She had to stay calm in order to get all the pieces of information from him. She would try hard to do the same with Alejandro if only the baby would calm down, too. The pain in her back made her feel like screaming.

"Tell me what you know," she demanded as she held on to her large belly. The pain was relieved a little by lifting it against the pressure of gravity.

"I'm sorry Agustina, I didn't mean to get into this subject now," Alejandro said apologetically. "Would you like to go back to bed and lie down?" He tried to change the subject, but Agustina was determined to hear what he knew.

"Tell me everything you know about Diego," she said. "I won't get up from here until you do." She moved the empty juice glass away and then rested her head on the table as she cried at the thought of her son. Agustina was ready to tell Alejandro that her son was really his son, too. As she lifted her head to face him she felt his hands on her tired back. He massaged her gently while he spoke.

"Dr. Tonami asked me to take samples of Diego's hair to the lab," he said softly.

"What hair samples?" Agustina asked. Her words were calm but her emotions were more agitated than the baby in her belly.

"When Dr. Tonami went to Mexico to see you after Diego died, he brought back hair samples from Diego's body," he explained. "I took the samples to the lab for analysis." He wanted to end the conversation there but could not think how to do it.

"What did the lab say about my son?" she asked. The day her son died kept playing in her mind over and over again like a broken record. *The mourning of a child never ends*, she thought.

"Please don't ask me to continue," he begged her. "This is not the right time for us to talk about such sad things."

"I can't have this baby until I hear what you have to say," she said, pushing herself up from her chair. Alejandro reached to help steady her, then put his arms around her. She was overwhelmed by his warmth and strength, and leaned into his embrace.

"Please tell me what you know about Diego."

Alejandro took a deep breath. "Diego was poisoned in Mexico," he said. Agustina thought her heart would burst with dismay. She began to feel faint, and a split second later, water like warm tea streamed down her short, swollen legs. She couldn't push away from Alejandro fast enough to keep it from soaking his pants. As for Diego, she knew what had happened. It was the mushroom. But what should she say? Agustina wanted to cry out loud from the anguish and from the rush of pressure bearing down against her legs.

"Oh my God! The baby's coming! Take me to the hospital," she ordered. "And please grab that small bag next to the bed." She pointed toward the bedroom, trying to hurry Alejandro. There was not much time; she could feel the baby pushing to get out.

Alejandro was visibly nervous. It was obvious to Agustina that he had not gone through this before. She had forgotten many things about pregnancy herself over the years, and recalled now that it had been Maki Tonami who drove her to the hospital and stayed with her when Diego was born. She was glad that this time, the child's father would be by her side.

Alejandro drove just like a detective through the streets of Los Angeles, taking shortcuts and back streets to reach the same hospital where Diego first entered the world. Agustina worried that Alejandro thought it was she who had fed Diego the poison mushroom, and she wondered why Dr. Tonami had never said anything to her about it.

But her thoughts were interrupted by the baby's insistent kicks. Her back ached, and she kept her legs close together and held on to her belly in hopes of slowing things down until they could get to the hospital.

"If the baby is a girl, I'd like to name her Lupita," she told Alejandro between contractions, hoping he would not object. She wanted to honor the Virgin of Guadalupe, who had supported and protected her through the long days of her pregnancy.

"What if it's a boy?" Alejandro asked as they pulled up to the hospital emergency entrance.

"I'd like him to be named after you," she said. She remembered the first time she had told him about the baby and how sure he was that it was not his child. But now Alejandro smiled from ear to ear.

The nurses at the hospital welcomed the couple inside and quickly helped Agustina onto a gurney covered with clean white sheets. She signed the required papers as they wheeled her into the delivery room.

Alejandro held her hand as the nurses helped her onto a birthing table under bright lights. Agustina was amazed at how things had changed since 1970, when Diego was born. The room was warmer and more comfortable. The table tilted her up somewhat so that she could easily put her feet in the stirrups and push down on them.

Hours went by and Agustina pushed until she thought she would faint. Alejandro mopped the perspiration from her face and encouraged her to keep trying. Nurses came and went, all with the same order: push. Finally, a doctor walked in and looked under the white sheets covering her knees.

"Agustina, you must push harder or I will have to take you in to surgery," he said sternly. Agustina could not understand why the baby would not come out. She had been so sure at home that the time had come. She didn't want to, but her back was hurting so much that she began to wail from the pain. She wondered if this agonizing delivery was a punishment for poisoning Diego. She would tell Alejandro the whole story as soon as the baby was born, she decided.

When another half-hour passed and the baby had not come, the doctor returned and asked the nurses to prepare Agustina for surgery. Alejandro kissed Agustina on the forehead and told her he would be waiting just outside.

"Don't worry," he assured her. "The doctor will take the baby so that you won't have any more pain."

"Thank you," she cried. An intravenous needle was inserted in her arm and a solution began to drip into her veins. Soon the bright lights overhead faded and Agustina drifted away in a peaceful sort of sleep. She looked forward to waking up to a new reality.

A healthy, robust baby boy cried out for his mother within another 30 minutes. But his mother was asleep and his father was the first to hold him.

"Mr. Sanchez, you have a son," the surgical nurse said as she swept into the waiting room with the little bundle in her arms. Alejandro held the infant in his large hands and rocked him tenderly back and forth, looking with amazement at the son he had thought he could never have.

"But the delivery was very hard on your wife, and we have moved her to the intensive care unit to monitor her closely," the nurse added almost instantly. "If you'll follow me, I'll show you where she is." A nurse's aide took the baby from Alejandro.

"What's wrong?" Alejandro asked as they walked through the hospital corridors.

"Agustina is in a coma," the nurse responded frankly.

"We've tried to awaken her but she's not responding. This pregnancy was very difficult for her at her age," she added. Tears ran down Alejandro's face and dripped off the ends of his mustache. He shook his head in disbelief. Agustina had seemed so well, and he had tried to take such good care of her. What went wrong? He hoped the sound of his voice would magically awaken her. He would tell her how much he loved her and their newborn baby boy.

The nurse showed Alejandro into a room full of machines and monitor and wires. In the midst of it all Agustina lay still on a bed. Her belly no longer looked as large, but her face was obscured by tubes connected to an electric device that pumped oxygen into her lungs. Alejandro could not believe what he saw. He knelt down at the side of the bed and prayed to Agustina's Virgin of Guadalupe to wake her up. He needed her and the baby needed his mother.

He stayed beside her until the floor nurses urged him to go home and get some rest. He gave them Agustina's home phone number to call if there was any news, as that is where he intended to stay. He wanted to be near Agustina's own statue of the Virgin, to pray to the saint that so often had given her courage.

He stopped at a pay phone on the way out to call his mother with the mixed news. She would pray, too, for Agustina, and reminded her son not to forget the newest member of the family in his distress. But the hope of a future with Agustina was waning inside Alejandro. He wished he could have done things differently. The streetlights blurred together through his tears.

As he entered Agustina's lonely home, he looked around at everything with a different perspective. He missed hearing her voice. He sat on the kitchen table, devastated and exhausted. Diego's eyes stared down at him from the photo on the wall. The boy looked so familiar to him. Perhaps he had interviewed him once, he thought.

In his work he had investigated many young men like Diego, but he realized that if he had ever met the boy he would also have met Agustina, and he would certainly have remembered her. He shook his head in confusion, and got up to begin cleaning the floor where Agustina's water had broken. He knew that he would have to call her family with the news and that they would come to see her, so he began to straighten up the kitchen in earnest. He pulled the tablecloth from the kitchen table and wrapped the wet towels from the floor inside it. He pulled out clean kitchen towels and then began to search the drawers for another tablecloth. Like his mother, Agustina had a junk drawer full of tools, matches, recipes and receipts, and when he opened it, some old photos of Diego caught his eye. Alejandro wondered why these particular photos were kept in a drawer, and assumed it was because Agustina studied them frequently. Ever the detective, Alejandro combed carefully through the stack of pictures, too. Why did Diego look so familiar?

Beneath a photo of Diego on vacation with the Tonami boys Alejandro found a snapshot of himself as a young Army recruit. *What is this doing here?* he wondered. *Did Mamá give this to Agustina? But why?* He remembered seeing the photo in one of his mother's albums, but he couldn't recall the setting. He was at a dance somewhere, wearing his dress uniform. He had his arm around a pretty girl as usual. He looked closely at the girl, trying to imagine why Agustina would have such a photo.

The truth struck him like a dagger: He was responsible for Agustina's eternal pain. Tears streamed down his face. He wanted so much to deny his presence in this snapshot of her past, yet it was plain to see that he was as guilty as any criminal he had ever investigated.

He turned to look at Diego's picture, and with a trembling

hand held the picture of Agustina and himself next to the one on the wall.

• • •

ALEJANDRO WOKE AT DAWN on an emotional roller coaster. As he hurried to the hospital, he planned what he would say to Agustina. He practiced out loud as he drove, but no matter how he approached it, nothing came out right.

The mood at the hospital was somber. Agustina had not made any progress during the night. The only sound in the room was the exhausted *whoosh* of the oxygen machine. Alejandro sat in a chair next to the bed and rested his head against Agustina's arm. He held her cool hand in both of his, feeling only a faint pulse.

Despondent, Alejandro stood up and walked to the nursery. His baby boy was filled with life. The contrast was almost too painful to bear, but the nurses were prepared for him and invited him into the nursery. They had him sit in a rocking chair and covered his clothing with clean towels, then handed him a warm, blue-and-white blanketed bundle. The baby settled easily into his father's strong arms. Alejandro tenderly rocked back and forth while the nurses prepared a bottle of formula.

Alejandro tipped the bottle toward his son's tiny lips, and as soon as the baby felt the warm nipple against his skin, he opened his mouth eagerly. Alejandro's pain ebbed and flowed with each breath the child took. He knew he could not cry. He had to be strong for his son's sake.

Soon the bottle was sucked empty and the baby's eyes had closed in peaceful sleep. Alejandro carefully tucked the child into his bassinet and walked back to Agustina's room.

The machine was still working her lungs for her. Her lips were dry and cracked. Why hadn't anyone told him that Agustina was pregnant after the dance? No one ever called or wrote him about her. But his connection to her, his friend Alfredo, had died in the war, and no one else would have known to tell him. He sat next to Agustina's bed and hung his head. She had always been such a strong woman. He hoped she would fight for her life now.

Alejandro began to speak softly to Agustina. He told her how sorry he was that he had not known about Diego. He described their son and told her how eager the baby was to meet his mother. In between sentences he looked hopefully for a flicker of recognition on her face, but Agustina looked far away and at peace.

Suddenly she seemed to gasp for air, and Alejandro felt her spirit leave her body. The various medical monitors began to sound their alarms. He could see that the technology was fighting to keep her and she was fighting to leave. He yelled for a nurse just as several rushed in the door.

They hurriedly fussed with various switches and buttons, but their efforts were futile. Agustina was gone. The machines stopped, leaving Alejandro with nothing but the sound of his own sobs. He wrapped her in his arms and pressed his ear to her heart, praying that she would revive.

"Agustina, I'm so sorry for the pain I've caused you," Alejandro cried. He held on to her tightly, wishing for her to reassure him but knowing well that her last breath had already seeped into his soul. A nurse patted him on the back as if to encourage him to rise to the occasion. Life still waited for him in the toothless smile of a newborn baby boy.

• • •